CRYSTAL FRAGMENTS

Betsy Ramsay

DEVORA
PUBLISHING
JERUSALEM • NEW YORK

Crystal Fragments
Published by Devora Publishing Company
Copyright © 2008 by Betsy Ramsay. All rights reserved.

COVER DESIGN: Zippy Thumim
TYPESETTING & BOOK DESIGN: Koren Publishing Services
EDITOR: Gila Green
EDITORIAL & PRODUCTION MANAGER: Daniella Barak

All rights reserved. No part of this book may be used or reproduced or transmitted in any form or by any means, electronic or mechanical, including photocopying, recording, or by any information storage and retrieval system, without written permission from the publisher.

Hard Cover ISBN: 978-1-934440-29-2

E-MAIL: sales@devorapublishing.com
WEB SITE: www.devorapublishing.com

Printed in Israel

DEDICATION

To my dear parents, Edith and George Waldbott, who by the quality of their daily lives, as individuals and as a team, were a beacon of light casting its broad beam upon my path and showing me the way.

•

I WISH I'D KNOWN HIM

I wish I'd known him.
I did in a sense
But only what my eyes told me.
My life was too busy
attracting the attention
    of the grown-ups
    to see the man
    beneath the face,
    perceiving behind his eyes,
    a heart too pure
    to acknowledge evil
    in his German neighbors.
They were Nazis,
"but only on the surface," he said,
and "Jews have always lived
in a hostile world,
sometimes more, sometimes less,
    so why stigmatize
    these quiet souls?"
But when his world fell apart
it broke his heart.
I wish I'd known my grandfather.

                              –Betsy Ramsay, 2006

TABLE OF CONTENTS

Introduction 1

Chapter I: The House in Flames 9

Chapter II: How Different Things Were Then! 17

Chapter III: Birthed in Brighter Days 35

Chapter IV: Desecration and Boyhood Passions 57

Chapter V: My Sons Depart 69

Chapter VI: Mocking Caricatures and "Racial Disgrace" .. 81

Chapter VII: Driven from Home 93

Chapter VIII: Boarding a Friendly Ship 105

Appendix I: Cornerstone-Laying Ceremony 115

Appendix II: Dedication Ceremony 119

Photographs 122

About the Author 127

INTRODUCTION

Jewish survivors often recount stories of horrific suffering during the Hitler period. This book, however, is the testimony of one German Jew who was rescued and protected by the very Nazis who sent others to their deaths. The story recorded here is an English adaptation of material that appears in teacher Leo Waldbott's account entitled: *"Mein Leben in Deutschland vor und nach dem 30, Januar 1933"* ("My life in Germany before and after January 30, 1933"). The purpose of his work was not so much to tell his personal story, but rather to describe the quality of life experienced by most German Jews in the years before and after Hitler's rise to power. He documented how, prior to the ignominious Hitler era, when their rights were whittled away to zero, the Jews of Germany held all the rights of ordinary German citizens and were often honored with high positions in government, culture, and society.

Interspersed within Leo Waldbott's story of his life in Germany are also excerpts from another account. His son George wrote several chapters, before he died, of an intended autobiography in which he described his own boyhood in Germany in the early twentieth century and his departure from the "homeland," in 1923. For the sake of the story, the excerpts from his account are included here as "journal entries."

Leo Waldbott taught Judaic studies to the Jewish children who attended the public schools of Speyer, Germany, from March 1890 until his retirement for health reasons in 1923. Besides serving as cantor and part-time rabbi in the Speyer synagogue, he devotedly poured his heart and soul into establishing a retirement home for the elderly Jews of the Pfalz, in the nearby city of Neustadt. He had the pleasure of participating in a dedication ceremony of the building project in which, with pomp and dignity, the mayor of Neustadt addressed the gathering, in September 1912. Only twenty-six years later he would have the heartbreak of watching this beloved home for the elderly meet a tragic demise as it burned to its foundations on the infamous day, November 10, 1938 – Kristallnacht. After the home was destroyed, Waldbott felt a driving sense of duty to record the story of the home for the elderly in its entirety. This, in turn, became a major thrust of his account.

It is of interest that at the time he left Germany, Leo Waldbott despaired of the home ever being rebuilt. Happily, it has been rebuilt on the same location but in a newer architectural design.

Leo Waldbott was my grandfather. Unfortunately, he met an untimely death a year and a half after successfully escaping the jaws of Nazi Germany. I knew him only superficially, as he died when I was a child of eight. I have only come to know him for the person he was in recent years through reading his own account of his life. My poem "I WISH I'D KNOWN HIM" reflects my sense of loss at not having known my grandfather better while he was alive.

Introduction

In this connection, please note that all three poems appearing in between the prose text were penned by the author and written simultaneously with the writing of this account, specifically for this story.

Leo Waldbott was a God-fearing man who, even in the face of Hitler's uncanny cruelty, never stopped loving "the Fatherland," which he persisted in seeing through "rose-colored lenses." He never spoke an unkind word about his fellow Germans.

Leo Waldbott and Hermine Rosenberger Waldbott had three children. Emil, the eldest (1891–1972), made his way to the "New World" in 1910 as an enterprising nineteen-year-old seeking his fortune. He tried his hand at various projects before settling into a partnership with his brother-in-law, in the soft drink industry. Although the sales figures of their company, Sweet Sixteen, never matched those of Coca-Cola or Vernors, Emil made a comfortable living for himself and his family. Helen Ullman, his first wife, bore him two healthy sons before her untimely death in 1923. His second wife, Lena Rosen, became a lifelong companion.

Leo and Hermine's second child was Elisabeth (born in 1893), better known as Friedl. She was a Down's Syndrome child and lived only to about twenty. She was tenderly cherished within the family circle.

The third child, George (1898–1982), was my father. He became a medical doctor and immigrated to the United States in 1923. No special presentation is needed, as excerpts from his journal appear generously throughout the upcoming story.

Unfortunately, I know practically nothing about my paternal grandmother, Hermine Waldbott, who died after complications from surgery at the young age of fifty-three. She must have been an unusually kind and tenderhearted person, and presumably neither my grandfather nor my father chose to speak much about her after her death, as neither ever got beyond their grief over her loss. Their prolonged silence, however, was a great pity. I would have dearly loved to know more about her, and readers might have liked to know, too.

Of special interest, however, are the measures my parents took to rescue Jews during the Hitler years. My father, unlike the majority of German Jews of the period, saw the handwriting on the wall early in 1933. In spite of their limited resources, my parents provided financial guarantees for a sizable number of the Jewish inhabitants of Speyer. Thanks to this measure, these fortunate ones gained permits to leave Germany while it was still possible for Jews to depart. They subsequently received asylum in our home in Michigan and were successfully rescued, one or two at a time, from the incinerators of Nazi Germany. Our home was a midway station where these refugees stayed until each could manage on his or her own.

When I am asked how this book came about, I recount the day in the fall of 1959, when, after moving from my husband's family estate in Sweden, I unpacked a carton bursting with papers and found, at the very bottom, a carbon copy of my grandfather's manuscript. As far as I know this was the only remaining copy. Yet to this day I have no idea how the papers got there. Finding the manuscript was something of a miracle.

The text was written in stilted, old-fashioned German and was hard to decipher. Yet between my dear now-deceased mother's persistence and my own growing interest in the subject matter, we succeeded in transforming the text into good, readable English. From that time on it was

Introduction

simply a step-by-step process of drawing from the material my grandfather had provided to put together this story.

The purpose of this book has been to make my grandfather's material more readily available for interested readers. The excerpts from my father's journals provide an added perspective and enrich the contents with expressive vignettes from the period.

CRYSTAL FRAGMENTS

Crystal fragments,
teardrops darting
from broken chandeliers,
splashing across
cobblestone alleys.
Rembrandts, Gauguins, Rubens
hurtling from high windows
shattering, scattering

and "the Beloved Child of the Pfalz,"
friendly harbor
for Jewish elderly –
how are they faring?

from billows of smoke
fiery serpents
raise
their noxious heads,
with venomous tongues
lashing this way and that.

and the fire trucks –
where are they?

CRYSTAL FRAGMENTS

will they come?
will they ever come
with hoses
to quell the blazing?

– Betsy Ramsay, 2005

CHAPTER ONE

The House in Flames

On November 10, 1938, a rude ringing struck terror into my slumber. I answered the phone.

"Mr. Waldbott! Is that you? The home for the elderly is in flames!" cried Dr. Strauss at the other end of the line.

Pulling up the blinds I viewed a heavy cloud of smoke erupting into a blood-red sky over the whole town of Speyer. Fires were everywhere.

My heart thumped. What was happening to the home for the aged that I had been first to propose as acting rabbi of the Speyer synagogue? The home was to become a "safe haven" for elderly Jews from all parts of the Pfalz, in the southwest corner of Germany. The idea was first proposed on October 12, 1907, and the home had become all we'd hoped for. But now, what was happening?

"What can we do to rescue our people? Can we get them out?"

"I don't know. I don't know," responded Dr. Strauss, the number-two man on the board of directors. "We must try!"

I would later learn what had happened earlier that morning to our cherished home for the Jewish elderly. A troop of armed men carrying axes, hammers, and pockettuls of matches had arrived at the home. They'd hacked an opening through the entranceway, chopped the great double doors to pieces, and set the drapery alight.

Billowing smoke soon filled the building. Then, racing through all the rooms, they screeched their war cry in the ears of sleeping residents:

"*Heraus!* [*Get out!*]"

Nor was the fire confined to the home for the elderly in Neustadt. The revered synagogues of Neustadt and Speyer were also set ablaze and burned swiftly to the ground. With the synagogue in Speyer, which I knew well, went a tastefully-furnished building, two Torah scrolls, a library of Jewish books, as well as a valuable collection of synagogue songs and music for choir and cantor – a treasure trove ravished by flames, in a moment.

Jumping out of bed at the first shout of alarm, most of the residents had hurriedly thrown on some clothes and fled to the nearby forest. Many were injured by glass splinters and were aching and covered with blood when they finally reached the woods. Not all of them reached the wooded area. Some were still in the house as flames wreaked havoc, rushing up the interior walls. While the beautiful home burned to the ground, the firemen did nothing.

As two of the elderly fled the building, Esther Lieberman called out to her companion, Sarah Klein:

"Why isn't the fire department here?"

"They are here! Open your eyes, Esther!"

"Why don't they put out the fire?"

"We're only Jews, dear! Run now! We must get out!"

"My hips won't take me. Ouch!"

By the time Dr. Strauss and I arrived at the home in Neustadt, nurse Else Mendelsohn was battling billowing smoke to rescue the residents. We found her in a room where two of the elderly were hurriedly throwing coats over their nightgowns.

"Ladies, you won't be returning! Put your clothes on! Dress properly!" Nurse Else insisted.

"Heraus!" bellowed a Nazi official. But Nurse Else stood her ground.

"I'm not leaving the building until all my people are dressed and brought to safety!"

"Well, see that you hurry!"

The next minute the Nazi's hard heart seemed to soften slightly.

"Don't you want to take anything? Jewelry or something?"

"You're not giving me time!"

"Go on! Take what you need, brave woman! I didn't know a Jew could be so brave!"

Finally, when everyone she could find was safely out, Nurse Else made her way through the suffocating clouds of smoke, breathing heavily.

Once she had caught her breath and was out of danger, she rounded up those who had not already fled and escorted these latecomers to the town tenement.

To my further sorrow, I would learn later that the destruction of the cherished home, affectionately known as the "Beloved Child of the Pfalz," had been declared "a work accident." The Nazi authorities had not wanted to burn the house down. They'd intended, instead, to snatch our lovely residence from us and let it serve as an Army administration building during a future war. But their henchmen perceived the home as a synagogue. After all, it had a prayer room, and their orders had been that all synagogues must go!

FLEEING AGAIN

It would have been anguish enough for our residents to have been granted refuge in the tenement where they fled, but worse was to come. The same day, all Jewish men of the province of Pfalz Rhineland, age sixteen to seventy, were arrested and taken to Dachau. The Pfalz was a large area, including the important towns of Kaiserlautern, Ludwigshafen, Mannheim, Heidelberg, and Neustadt, as well as Mainz, Speyer, and Worms, known for the brutal slaughter of thousands of Jewish inhabitants in 1096 during the First Crusade.

All of our people who had lived in the home were over seventy, so no one was taken. Yet they, too, were subjected to a harsh decree. Our board of directors received their orders from the regional leader, Buerkel:

"All Jews out of town and out of the region by nightfall!"

Those not herded as cattle onto freight trains were commanded to leave their dwellings – homes that might have served the family for generations. The whole of the Pfalz Rhineland was to be emptied of Jews. All in one day!

Many of the residents of our home were riddled with ailments. Some could no longer think clearly. How many would be up to a second desperate flight? None of us dared ask. And the authorities certainly weren't asking. They wouldn't have minded if we'd all died in flight. Ninety-eight-year-old Rosa Cohn did, in fact, perish due to the pressures. Rosa was a special lady. She had been the first to move into our beloved home at its opening on the memorable date of April 1, 1914.

Yet someone did care. Nurse Else willingly took up the ponderous task of corralling her "chicks" and redirecting each person, one by one, to a safe haven. Some, nonetheless, went astray, as in the case of Sarah Klein and Esther Lieberman.

The House in Flames

As the morning wore on with the odor of burned bricks and mortar hanging heavy in the air, Sarah Klein and Esther Lieberman had made their way, puffing and panting, to a public park off the main thoroughfare of town. Esther, almost stone deaf, and Sarah, whose eyesight was failing, had missed Nurse Else's order to proceed to the tenement. In the confusion they had lost track of their faithful nurse. When word went out that all Jews must leave the region, their ears had not picked that up either.

Esther and Sarah found a quiet place in the park and simply sat there on a wooden bench in a daze, not knowing where to turn. They were still there when a Nazi gendarme came along and poked them with his baton.

"What are you two doing? Get on home! No loitering!"

"We haven't any home, officer. It was burned down this morning."

"No home? Burned down?"

"And the firemen didn't take out their hoses. Why didn't they?"

"I'm sorry, but we don't allow loitering."

"Where should we go?"

"We've walked this far and gotten nowhere."

"Ah! It's the old folks' home for Jews?"

They both nodded.

"No relatives to help you?"

"No one in Neustadt," Sarah answered, dejected.

"I don't know anyone in this city," Esther sighed.

"Well, if you're from that home get into the car! Get in quickly!" he ordered, butting them roughly again with the baton and shoving them both into the back of the vehicle. Then the engine rumbled to a start.

"Where are we going?"

13

"I don't usually help Jews," he muttered. "You're probably some of the people who scattered after the fire. Nurse Mendelsohn is looking for you. She's a Jew, but a good woman."

With that he drove off. Before long, Esther and Sarah were reunited with Nurse Else and the troubled group.

NAMES ASSIGNED BY CITY CLERK

The story you are reading is my story, and my name is Leo Waldbott. You've read the tale of how our cherished home for the elderly perished under the Nazis – the home which had begun as an idea in my heart and was first presented to the board for our choir in the synagogue of Speyer on October 12, 1907.

I am the same Mr. Waldbott whom every Jewish schoolchild in Speyer will remember. I taught Judaism to all the children from the 120 Jewish families in Speyer, which they studied in addition to the required subjects in the public schools.

In my story I will reveal something of the quality of life for Jews in Germany as compared with their fellow citizens before and after *der Führer* came to power on January 30, 1933.

I come from a long line of teachers, hailing back to 1748 in the records of the Rhine/Pfalz. My father, Lazarus, was a teacher who died in 1869. I was only two at the time, and my grandfather, the teacher Levi Waldbott, and his wife took me into their home in the small village of Steinbach. I became the youngest family member in a household with seven "brothers and sisters," who were actually my aunts and uncles.

My grandfather's salary from the municipality came to a maximum of sixty gulden per year, a very meager sum. Yet he managed to provide each of his children with a higher education. I don't know how he did it. I and my three "brothers" became teachers and my four "sisters" entered other professions.

I married my dear wife, Hermine, in 1890. Her father, too, was a teacher. Hermine and I were happy together during all thirty years of our marriage, until she died in connection with surgery, in 1920.

It's interesting how our family received the name Waldbott. When the Pfalz became French in 1804, Napoleon required all Jews on the left bank of the Rhine to take German names. In 1806, within two years after Napoleon took command in the Rhineland, the Jews of Steinbach were summoned to the office of the mayor. There a clerk opened a page at random from the school textbook, *The Rhine River*. As he read aloud from the book, every appropriate noun was assigned to a family in the order of its appearance in the story – becoming names such as Rheinström [the Rhine River], Brunehild [a woman's name], and Eichhold [a kindly oak].

When the city clerk came to our family he read: "The river flows by the castle of Count Waldbott von Bassenheim." So the name we received was more than an ordinary noun. It was the name of a family of German nobility.

A gravestone built into the wall of the time-honored Dome of Speyer (the Kaiserdom) is inscribed: "Count Waldbott von Bassenheim, Bishop of Worms and Speyer." Thus we know that one Count Waldbott was also a bishop of the church and that he must have died between the years 1030 and 1060, when the Kaiserdom was built by Emperor Konrad II. At least two branches of Count Waldbott's family still exist, one in Holland and one in Hungary.

CHAPTER TWO

How Different Things Were Then!

The old method of education in the religious schools contributed to good mutual understanding among the local peoples of different backgrounds. This system was still in effect in two towns in the Pfalz, Speyer and Pirmasens, in the 1870s and later.

There were fifty small Jewish grade schools in the area as well as the Baermann'sche educational establishment in Bad Durkheim, from which the six-year, non-classical secondary school later derived.

Children representing all the prevalent religious groups – Catholic, Protestant, and Jewish – were enrolled in these public schools. The same general subjects were taught to all. Religious education was taught in the middle schools and high schools, and it was only for these classes that the different religious groups were separated.

I graduated from the Protestant Teachers' Seminary in Kaiserslautern on July 31, 1885. At first I found work as an interim principal of a Jewish school in Hagenbach. Besides teaching twenty-five pupils, I conducted synagogue services in the town. Then, after four and a half years, I completed some supplementary studies and began work as a public school teacher in Speyer, on March 1, 1890. This was the beginning of what would become my life's calling.

At first I taught sixty children in one of the city school buildings and got along well with my colleagues. The intimate friendships I enjoyed with many of them have, in fact, weathered the havoc of Hitler's cruel regime.

All these institutions, including the Jewish schools, were funded by the government, and local communities raised support for some of our materials. Peaceful cooperation and mutual respect were a common denominator. This included religious schools. In this connection my "Christian" colleagues at times commented to me about my much esteemed predecessor, Mr. Schloss. "So-and-so studied under Mr. Schloss," one would tell me, and I knew he meant the student had received excellent instruction.

My younger son, George, keeps a journal, parts of which he has generously shared with me. In it he writes about my religion classes, and my heart is warmed to see that he enjoyed them. This was not immediately apparent at the time:

> [The classes were] extremely fascinating and covered many subjects. We learned how, after the destruction of the Second Temple, Jews went to North Africa, Spain, and other parts of Europe, and there maintained their cultural and religious identity, although scattered far and wide. We learned of the severe suffering of our people during the Spanish Inquisition and about the pogroms in Germany in the time of the great plague, when Jews were accused of poisoning the wells with deadly germs and causing suffering and death for many. We were told that the towns of Speyer, Worms, and Mainz were

the centers of Jewish civilization as well as the locations for infamous ghettos where Jewish homes were burned, their children murdered, and where those who remained were driven from their homes. On the other hand, our people were at times regarded as useful to the state because of their intellectual gifts. During periods of economic distress they would be recalled from their exile to the towns of Speyer, Worms, and Mainz to help governing bodies restore financial stability.

I taught about great Jewish men such as Maimonides, the renowned physician, and among the German Jews – Spinoza, the philosopher, Mendelsohn the musician, and Heine, the poet. I particularly enjoyed expounding for the children on how the Jews of Germany acquired political and civil equality with all other Germans.

As early as the seventeenth century the great reformer and philosopher, Moses Mendelsohn, a friend of the poet Lessing, laid the foundation for the liberation of his people from the shackles of ghetto life. Others such as Gabriel Riesser and Bismark later finished the job, until every Jew in Germany was a free man, enjoying equality with all other citizens!

The Jewish people of the Pfalz had considerable economic freedom in the mid-1800s, and by the end of the Franco-Prussian War in 1871, they received full equality with all Germans. They were active in the retail wine and tobacco trade in the mountain region of the "Haardt." Elsewhere they traded successfully in cattle and vegetable products, and did well in the whole region.

As for me, personally, I was fortunate enough to be able to build my own home in the late 1890s, shortly after arriving in the town of Speyer, where Hermine and I would raise our family. Owning one's own home was the primary goal of even the poorest among the people in those days. Whatever money was left after daily household expenses was stored away as savings in some form whether at home or in the bank, lest it be "wasted on newfangled conveniences."

The town of Speyer had been laid out without any real plan. Many narrow, winding lanes branched out in all directions, with the hub of their connecting spokes converging at Main Street. The larger streets, however, were parts of main arterial roads leading out of town toward the surrounding cities: Worms and Ludwigshafen in the north, Heidelberg across the Rhine to the east, and Germersheim and Strasbourg to the south. The farther one proceeded from the center of town, the straighter and wider the streets and the more modern the homes became. Our house was at the end of town on one of the newer streets, Landauerstrasse.

In one of his journal entries my son George nostalgically describes our home on Landauerstrasse:

> The house was two stories high and built of red sandstone. The attic area housed my older brother and me as well as two or three boarders.
>
> Like most of the residences in town, ours had a small garden in back, which was my father's pride. A garden house, some benches, and a table, all made of sandstone, stood in its center near the big pear tree.
>
> To fertilize the pear tree we would dig a small ditch around the tree every fall and give it a few bucketsful of the precious contents of our sewage system. Thanks to this practice we would harvest

How Different Things Were Then!

more and bigger pears each year, and I was sure they were also more delicious. The constant care that we lavished on the beautiful rosebushes and fuchsia shrubs of every possible variety constituted a vital part of our daily lives. Father also had an impressive collection of rare cactus plants in the garden.

The sewage system was one of the old-fashioned features of our town. A large cement tank built into the ground behind the house was located near the entrance to the garden. Once a month the so-called "city guard" would draw up with four to six horse-drawn tank wagons and another wagon on which the pumping mechanism for clearing out waste from the tank was mounted. It was only at these times that the sweet scent of the roses and the fragrance of the flowering trees were blotted out by the reeking odor of sewage wastes – an unpleasant but necessary evil.

The city-owned equipment was a daily sight on the streets of Speyer. The contents of the tanks played a valuable role for farmers at a time when the cost of commercial fertilizers was out of reach. Farmers were willing to pay the municipality dearly for this precious stuff that would stimulate the growth of their potatoes and grain. This also helped maintain the city's treasury.

And then there was the old lamplighter! The streetlamp in front of the house would be lit each evening by a man carrying a big pole over his shoulder. We children enjoyed watching him hurry along, stop for a minute at our lamppost, and then hurry away to the next one. There were only two lamplighters in town, and the procedure had to be performed quickly as the city's gas was too precious to be wasted.

PRIDE AND INSULTS

In addition to teaching, as a Jewish teacher I carried out important functions in the synagogue. My duties usually included all the tasks performed by the rabbi: conducting religious services in the town on Saturdays and holy days, holding bar mitzvah classes, officiating at wedding and burial ceremonies, visiting the sick, administering charitable projects, and others.

In connection with my duties as a teacher, George recounts in his journal a matter about which I rarely spoke at home. Yet both my sons, George and Emil, knew about it. This concerned my relationship with my boss over many years – a matter that caused me great personal hardship:

> Years ago, as a young man coming from the small village of Hagenbach, Father applied for the teaching position he would hold for over twenty-five years. At this time a little incident occurred that made things very difficult for him. He and two other contestants had to perform synagogue services in a competitive trial. Father's voice, according to everyone who heard him, was by far the best. His sermon was considered the most inspiring of the three.
>
> After the services, Mr. Hertz, the perennial president of the congregation, received the three for an interview at his home. Father did not appear

in striped pants and tailcoat like the other contestants. The young village teacher neither knew about this custom, nor did he have the financial means to buy such an outfit. Mr. Hertz's ego was hurt and he voted against him. Yet the other members of the board overruled the president. Thus Father obtained the position against Mr. Hertz's will, which only added insult to injury for this prideful man.

For more than twenty-five years father suffered the ill-effects of his impropriety. He was personally blamed for the ignominious defeat of the candidate of Mr. Hertz's choice, and the boss tried to get even with him on every occasion. He held down his salary whenever the question of a raise came up and prohibited any progressive measure which father tried to introduce into the services.

What was worse for a man of German background, he worked on Father's sense of pride. Father "was only a servant to the congregation and to its president." He was expected to show Mr. Hertz deference and to obey him at all times. Father, for his part, was held in high esteem in the community both as a teacher and a minister of the Jewish faith, and he was a strong-minded individualist himself. Therefore, many clashes ensued between Father and the boss.

DER FÜHRER'S RISE TO POWER

In view of what would be the ominous consequences of der Führer's rise to power, I, Leo, feel it my duty to give a brief account of what was going on politically during that period. In the early 1930s, Germany was thrust into the depression that had begun earlier in America. By 1933, nearly one-third of the German labor force was unemployed. Already in 1930, the Nazis, the most vociferous political entity, made enormous gains in the parliamentary elections, with their representation in the Reichstag, Germany's parliament, rising from 12 to 107.[1] In the election two years later, as they rallied around Adolf Hitler, their representation grew even stronger.

Following this election, Hitler was offered the vice-chancellorship, but he was hungry for total power and declined the offer. Shortly thereafter, he was offered the chancellorship, but with certain limitations. He again declined.

By January 1933, people were feeling that Germany needed a strong leader who could deal with the growing political unrest and provide relief from the depression. Adolf Hitler made far-reaching promises of welfare and employment for all, and these held great appeal. People reached out eagerly for what they hoped would be the answer to their needs. Unfortunately for all, Hitler never followed through with these promised reforms, and yet, at this juncture, he was awarded the full chancellorship for which he had been holding out. Thus the era of the oppressive Third Reich began.

POSITIONS OF TRUST

My sphere of influence was considerable before the changes that came about in 1933. I want to tell about this, not to exalt

---

[1]. "Nazism... was [initially] a... combination of various ideologies and groups, centered around anger at the Treaty of Versailles and what was considered to have been a Jewish/Communist conspiracy to humiliate Germany at the end of the First World War." Quoted from Wikipedia Encyclopedia. (Compare to comments by Leo and journal entry from George in Chapter Three, "Tactics of the Overlords" section.

myself but simply to cast light on the relationships that prevailed under the old regime between Christian and Jewish people. The distinctions of Aryan and non-Aryan were not used until the "new era" of Hitler.

The versatility of my occupation gave me a high income for that time: 7,000 marks (M) per year. After my retirement from service in the school in 1923 for health reasons, this income was reduced to about 4,000 M.[2]

In 1911, by decree of the reigning Prince Luitpold of Bavaria, I was promoted to *Hauptlehrer* (head teacher), and in 1916 I was again promoted, this time to *Oberlehrer* (supervising teacher). This also meant additional income. Later, on my seventieth birthday, I was further honored in the synagogue in Speyer when the regional rabbi bestowed on me the honorable title of "Chover."[3]

I also held a position of great trust for many years on the board of trustees for the governmental Teachers Pension Fund Society. For this society I examined accounts and allocated special funds.

In the congregation, where I served as cantor until 1921, there were about 500 Jewish souls out of a total population of 20,000 in Speyer. After retiring as cantor I continued serving as choir director and organist.

Besides acting as chairman of the Jewish teachers' and cantors' club for twenty-five years, I was a member of the

---

2. Seven thousand marks would have corresponded to $20,160 per year in the currency of the time, and M 4,000 to $11,520. Bearing in mind the relative cost for consumer goods then, even the lesser of these two sums would have been an attractive salary as a bar of Palmolive soap would have cost 3 cents then, a pair of all-leather shoes one dollar, and a pair of flannel trousers $1.16!
3 "Chover" is a Hebrew word meaning friend or member.

executive board of that club under the German Reich government. During this period, when an insurance plan for Jewish teachers and their dependents was enacted, I was elected treasurer of this agency. Nonetheless, inflation gradually took the upper hand in Germany, and when funds gave out completely, insurance benefits ceased.

JEWS DIED FOR FATHERLAND

Politically, the Jewish people in the Pfalz were never conspicuous. Most kept their liberal democratic views and exercised the right to vote for as long as they could without registering as members of the National Socialist Party. A small number of the 9,650 Jews in the Pfalz were Social Democrats. None were active as Communists, and only a few belonged to the Communist Party in the period between 1910 and 1933.

Over the years, Jewish men in Speyer held honorary positions in the town councils and posts as managers of banks and commercial enterprises. They enjoyed warm recognition among the population, which even the harshest measures during the Hitler regime couldn't wipe out.

Yet nowhere in the Pfalz was there an environment where Zionism flourished. Instead, Jewish people were ready to live and die "for the Fatherland." Thirteen Jewish men from Speyer gave their lives in battle during World War 1. These represented 6.5 percent of the entire Jewish community, which by this time had dwindled to 200 souls. A memorial would have been built in the synagogue to honor these men who had made the ultimate sacrifice for their country. Instead the synagogue itself was destroyed on the sinister date of November 10, 1938.

> Though people may be very near one another
> in their thoughts,

they may collide with an impact
when the action starts.

– *Author unknown*

MILITARY SPLENDOR

The German Army held great appeal also for my two sons. George, the youngest, was an impressionable lad who idealized the army in its military splendor. He, too, would have been ready to die for his country. In fact, he came very close to doing this when his entire unit was wiped out during World War I. He would have, doubtless, perished with the others had he not been admitted to the Army infirmary a day or two earlier for severe influenza.

George writes in his journal about his sentiments as a young boy when he frequently viewed the military displays from our front window:

> From the far end of the street we could see the permanent quarters of the Second Bavarian Engineering Battalion. Had we ever planned to sell our home, this feature alone would have brought up its value at least 100 percent.
>
> The military life and activities of this battalion were an integral part of the development of our town. The younger generation was particularly affected. How often we watched from our windows as squads of soldiers fell into the goose-step for the salute of a higher officer passing their way!
>
> On Sundays the Catholic members of the battalion marched toward our home in their spotless, blue uniforms to the strains of famous German marches. An hour later the Protestant members

would march by with the same flare and decorum. This same marching music would in time come to be adopted by military bands around the world.

The band in which my brother, Emil, also participated, was headed by a brilliant musician. We could hear the most delightful concerts when the band serenaded the wives of officers in front of their homes. After the church services on Sundays and on Saturday afternoons they would play in the marketplace or the Dome Park that surrounded the old cathedral.

Men and women of the town, particularly the younger set, would parade back and forth, listening to the music. Of course, the fellows would be hoping to meet members of the fairer sex among the crowd. Many a romance was birthed at these concerts!

These events fostered love for good music among the young folks, as well. Operas of Wagner and works of Mozart, Schubert, and other classical composers were initially presented to us by this band in our childhood. The "more modern" compositions of Lehar and the Strausses were also presented. Each of these compositions would then be performed over and over.

Once a year the battalion built a nearly mile-long pontoon bridge. The soldiers exhibited top efficiency, thoroughness, and obedience to superiors as they completed this temporary bridge across the Rhine in just a few hours.

Other days we boys would follow the soldiers into the forest and watch them fell trees and build

How Different Things Were Then!

dams, railroads, and wooden bridges across small rivers. We would sneak up on them at target practice and witness their attacks on an artificial fortress on the outskirts of town.

Other military regiments were also delegated to Speyer to learn the art of building pontoon bridges. The orange uniforms of the cavalry, the light blue of the infantry, the green of the chasseur, and the navy blue of the artillery sparked the whole town with color and brought in new vitality.

When we boys would go hiking and pass the barracks of the Second Bavarian Engineering Battalion, we would peer into the warehouses and marvel. Pride in our country filled us with confidence as we viewed evidence of Germany's peacetime preparedness.

Here were vehicles loaded with pontoons, boats, and all materials necessary for building bridges. We saw the field kitchens with cases of canned food and other provisions lined up in perfect order. There were neat piles of guns and bayonets, large stores of blankets, and new, grey field uniforms which, in contrast to the bright colors of the marching battalions, presented an ominous sight.

For the young people the military spectacles, parades, and band concerts were the football and baseball events of our day. Wherever people met informally they loved discussing play-by-play accounts of each event. The feats of the military were the highest achievements in our eyes. Its officers were put on a pedestal as objects of hero worship for boys and girls.

We were told that in an emergency it would require no more than three hours to have the whole battalion ready to move to the French frontier. With typical German thoroughness, even railroad cars had been specifically designated, some for men and some for material.

On July 13, 1914, World War I was declared, and that fearful day of emergency actually arrived. No German youth had stopped to consider at the time that the very preparedness we were so proud of might contribute to the fears and jealousies of our French neighbors and help trigger the onset of war. We were only thinking of defending our democracy against French aggression.

THE KAISER COMES TO TOWN

George continues reminiscing:

> Once during my childhood the Kaiser and his entourage made a public appearance in our neighborhood. One morning we looked out the window and saw an array of technicians, guards, military police, and all kinds of vehicles on the road. Behind them followed scores of special artillery and cavalry detachments. Next we watched as hundreds of generals and high officers passed on horseback. Brilliantly colored feathers on their helmets floated in the breeze. The armor of the cavalry shone brightly and swords glittered as the officers trotted elegantly on their thoroughbreds. We beheld the magnificent sight in wide-eyed wonder.

How Different Things Were Then!

When the great warlord himself appeared high up astride his marvelous steed, talking and gesturing to his generals, I was thrilled beyond words. I had an urgent desire to get right in there, to join these valiant men, though I was only ten.

I would, of course, have to wait. Not until after graduation from high school would I be old enough to wear the epaulettes of an officer and carry an officer's sword. And first I would have to begin as a private. Yet thoughts of the healthful exercise, the training in subordination, the camaraderie of the Army praised by German poets, and above all an ardent love for country quickened a burning desire in me to be a soldier some day.

SURVIVORS BROUGHT TO MANNHEIM

Now, I, Leo, will return to the events following the shameful destruction of our home for the elderly, which we had affectionately nicknamed the "Beloved Child of the Pfalz." The good news was that everyone found in the building left safely, thanks to Nurse Else's clear thinking. Yet, sadly, two occupants, Frau Camilla Haas and Fanny Bender, were not found. We may never know whether or not they perished in the flames.

Nurse Else escorted the residents of the fire-ravaged building whom she had helped escape by train to the Jewish community of Mannheim. These traumatized people received care and doctoring for their wounds there.

The Jewish hospital and nursing home could adequately accommodate some, and a small number were taken in by relatives.

Still, there were a considerable number with no place to go – many more than the hospital and nursing home could normally receive. Yet the administration of the nursing home knew how to fit many into small quarters, and a way was found to give shelter and care to all the remaining refugees. Each poor soul received a bed somewhere in the building. At the same time, the limited space for beds and household items created great hardship.

The crowded conditions were reminiscent of the sufferings and miseries of our people during times of persecution in the Middle Ages, during the thirteenth and fourteenth centuries, when Jews in Germany were plundered and hunted down like wild animals. At that time many were forced to flee for their lives or risk being burned alive by the populace.

By contrast, the harsh circumstances our people were forced to cope with were only slightly less severe. Fortunately, however, these were partially alleviated a few weeks later when the administration in Mannheim were able to rent a house under Jewish auspices that provided more room temporarily for our people. Those who had survived the trauma of past weeks remained in the care of Else Mendelsohn. The former supervising nurse, Carola Adler, who had served faithfully since the home was first furnished over twenty-five years earlier, had departed on November 10.

Even when the crushing hardship of Kristallnacht was behind us and our aging Jewish population had been deprived by the fire of security and peaceful surroundings for their last years, a further harsh measure added salt to our wounds. After all the destruction of our property that fateful night, the administration of our home was required to clean up the rubble. We were also to pay the costs of leveling the ground after the fire. Incredible! Yet I have the proof of it. The annual financial statement for 1938–39 shows this expense amounted to RM 1,200.

I wonder if the welfare institution and the Beloved Child of the Pfalz will ever be rebuilt. We doubt it, in view of the harsh conditions that have been thrust upon the Jews in Germany during this century of "enlightenment." The majority of our fellow believers, the young people in particular, have left the homeland where their forefathers had been able to live happy and prosperous lives. Who will still be there to build the home up again?

CHAPTER THREE

Birthed in Brighter Days

Things had been so different when plans for building the home were birthed. The year was 1907, and I was a member of the board for the choir through my rabbinical responsibilities in the synagogue. At the close of our board meeting on October 12, the floor was opened for members to bring up suggestions. I rose to my feet and proposed this project. The issue was the urgent need for a care facility for lonely and elderly believers in our community. Nothing of this kind existed in the whole area of the Pfalz up to that time, and many of the younger families had no way of giving proper care to their elderly parents and close relatives.

Mr. Isador Rose, our director of the board for the choir, enthusiastically agreed, and the board voted unanimously to follow up on my proposal. From that moment preparations for founding the home were on their way.

We held our first general planning meeting on April 26, 1908, in the Saal building in Neustadt, on the Haardt River. The turnout exceeded our wildest dreams. Over a hundred representatives from all congregations of the Pfalz were present, and they arrived from elsewhere as well. The press also reported favorably on the event.

A marvelous spirit of unity became the emblem that day for the home's existence. Our hearts were full of confidence. When a good purpose binds people together in a single-hearted endeavor, great things happen.

In the work of promoting and financing, commitment was strong. There was a moving spirit of cooperation. No faint-heartedness here! All were eager to play a part in this first welfare project that the Jewish people of the Pfalz could call their own.

In 1910, at the second meeting of the association for founding the home, I, as treasurer, showed assets of M 125,500[4]. The project experienced such an increase in funds that the target date set for building was pushed forward.

Next a committee was elected to find a site. Property offers were made by five different cities in the Pfalz. During this search we were always well received by the authorities: mayors, city councilors, and building inspectors.

AN OUTRIGHT GIFT

In Neustadt we were conducted from the railroad station up the gentle incline of Karolinenstrasse, past many beautiful villas. The city of Neustadt offered us a site as an outright gift! The property had a frontage of eighty meters and was sixty meters in depth. From the position where the home would stand, a marvelous view carried the eye to the wooded heights across the way. To the east another panoramic vista opened across the city, as far as the plains of the Rhine River. The city park bordered the property's south side.

The third official gathering became a milestone in the history of our home. Approximately 550 members of the

---

4. This amount was equivalent to $31,375, which is approximately $433,600 in terms of today's purchasing power.

extended committee for establishing the home, from all parts of the Pfalz, Frankfurt, and Mannheim, etc., gathered in the large meeting hall. A vote was taken, and although there were several other possibilities, an overwhelming majority voted to accept the splendid gift offered by the city of Neustadt.

The mayor of Neustadt was informed by telegram, and a genial meeting followed at the Hotel Eintracht.[5] Rabbi C. Seligmann of Frankfurt gave a memorable speech thanking the city authorities and closed with a toast to the mayor. Mayor Wand then returned his toast, praising our oneness of spirit.

THE FINEST DRAWING

At the general meeting that followed, the building inspector, Mr. Sternlieb from Ludwigshafen, submitted a plan to our board of trustees. By public announcement, all architects of the Pfalz as well as those from Frankfurt and Mannheim were to be invited to participate in a competition for the best building plan. This course of action was readily accepted. A prize of M 2,200 would be divided among three top contestants.

The committee of judges consisted of seven members. They were to work together with Mr. Ullman of the Speyer Building Authority, whose freely offered help lightened our workload considerably. He helped to designate the judges and welcome entries into the competition.

We had been told by several experts to expect only a few entries, but remarkably the enthusiastic involvement of the honored Professor Hoffman resulted in fifty-eight excellent project drawings being entered in the competition.

---

5. Eintracht is the German word for "harmony."

The drawings were displayed in a large hall in Speyer, and from them the judges selected a winning entry and two runners-up.

The prize-winning drawing was of distinctly higher quality than all the others. Designed by the architect Senf, the sketch was entitled "House and Garden." It was marked by simplicity and expressed well the desired character of the home. Its design promoted a peaceful and friendly atmosphere while also meeting the requirements of the building plan.

Since the architect Senf was from Frankfurt on the Main River and of the other winners were also contestants from outside the Pfalz, the committee bought three entry sketches from local architects and awarded each a sum of M 125.

Construction was scheduled to take one year, beginning in June 1912. The rough structure would be ready within six months at an estimated cost of M 156,800, and this figure was accepted by the committee.

CORNERSTONE LAID

On September 29, 1912, an impressive cornerstone-laying ceremony was held for the home as the initial step toward construction of the "Beloved Child of the Pfalz." Flags flew with Germany and Bavaria's traditional colors. Crowds filled the Karolinenstrasse as more and more busloads of people arrived.

Among the guests of honor conducted to the podium was Mayor Wand of Neustadt. His presence there as well as that of a government official, Mr. Junker, and the district physician, Dr. Spenkuch, both representatives of the royal household, gave the sanction of the State. Also escorted to the podium were a member of the Bavarian legislature and

Birthed in Brighter Days

certain church officials. The presence of the latter signified "peace and harmony" between our two religions. Men and women by the hundreds flanked the podium on either side.

The chairman of the committee opened the festive occasion with a word of welcome to each of the honored guests, expressing great appreciation to the municipality of Neustadt for their generous gift of property. This, he maintained, created "a bond between us and ties that held promise of peace for all time to come."

The men's choir sang "Holy is the Lord," by Schubert, and a number of speeches followed. Mayor Wand stated on behalf of the city administration that as soon as the plan for erecting a home for elderly Jewish people became known, the public offices of various cities had wanted to get involved. Each desired to extend some help toward this welfare undertaking. His own administration saw it as an opportunity to promote a spirit of freedom and tolerance where all may live side by side in mutual self-respect. During all his eight years as mayor, he said, he hadn't witnessed a better attended event.

Rabbi Steckelmacher gave the dedication of the foundation stone. He asked the blessing of the Almighty upon our aged regent, Prince Luitpold of Bavaria, upon our homeland, and upon the people of Neustadt:

"May we all continue, as in the past, to live together in neighborly love despite our differences in religion. Let us all remain true to the Jewish people and to the homeland as well!"

This was recorded in a document which Rabbi Steckelmacher first read and then inserted in the foundation stone, to be buried. While he was reading aloud, enthusiastic pounding of hammers in the customary fashion resounded through the crowd. Even the rabbi participated, adding his hammering to the rest.

Mayor Wand then spoke:

"For the elderly, a beloved and peaceful home, for the lonely, help and support and a new domicile, and for the cause of harmony and mutual tolerance, an honorable memorial for our entire citizenry."

With the song "We believe, one and all, in only one God," the men's choir brought the celebration to a close.

A DAY LIKE NONE OTHER

In the spring of 1914 we had the joy of seeing the house emerge as a testimony to the artistic and practical ability of our construction crew and all who had participated. The home was officially opened on April 1, a day like none other.

There was great activity in the home and surrounding neighborhood as the day of the official dedication ceremony approached. By that time, due to the urgency of the need, seven residents had already moved in. The memorable ceremony would crown six years of work by the Jewish people of the Pfalz.

A local newspaper, the Pfälzer Kurier, wrote:

> May 10 [1914] was the important day for the opening and dedication of the Hebrew home for the elderly. The home now stands complete after six years of preparation and two years of construction work. Not only did the people of Neustadt celebrate, but Jews from all parts of the Pfalz participated in the celebration, arriving with early morning trains by the hundreds. Toward eleven A.M., cars, buggies,

and pedestrians were flocking in the direction of the beautifully located home. The building itself was tastefully decorated with flags and garlands. White-and-blue flags along with the black-white-and-red flags could be seen flying from a distance. Girls dressed in white flanked the steps.

In the terrace room of the home, fenced off for the occasion, the guests of honor began arriving. Among them: the honorable Mayor Wand, Mr. Jos. Wolff, a church elder of Bavaria, the district official, Mr. Junker, Mr. Tisch, the court director, Mr. Limbacher, a revenue officer, and numerous city council members as well as architects and others who had been actively involved.

Here are a few highlights[6] from that memorable event: The ceremony opened with a choral piece by the band of the Eighteenth Infantry Regiment from Landau, conducted by Mr. Wolter. Next, music director Mr. Stahl energetically conducted a combined choir from the synagogues of Neustadt, Landau, Speyer, and Rülzheim, singing "The Glory of God in All Nature."

Mr. Max Wolff presented a poetic prologue, and the dedication and blessing upon the house were pronounced by Rabbi Dr. B. Einstein of Landau

THE SILVER KEYS

Following the music and words of dedication, a keychain with silver keys was presented to the aged acting president, Mr. Sigmund Herz, from Speyer. With keys in hand he

---

6. For a more detailed account see Appendix II.

CRYSTAL FRAGMENTS

ceremoniously unlocked and opened the front door. He then crossed the threshold and the home was officially opened. Against the background of festive musical tones of the harmonium, 530 guests eagerly entered and viewed our elegantly furnished building.

The dedication dinner was held in the Saalbau Hall and a gala ball followed. At the dinner Mayor Wand was first to address the guests. The mayor emphatically stated that residents at our home were every bit as important as every other citizen and thereafter followed a hearty applause.

From subsequent table speeches I will only quote Rabbi Weil of Kaiserlauten:

> "Producing this home for the elderly is twice as valuable a project as demanding equal rights for our Jewish people. Such an accomplishment provides legitimacy for the political fight for equal rights. You who have born the responsibility for this project have translated our common thinking into a vital deed of mercy. I therefore propose a toast to all parties who have worked here together in harmony!"

The first three or four years of strong National Socialist presence in the government passed relatively well. We were in no way disrupted in the operations of our facility. They had no time yet to bother with us

After 1933, when Adolf Hitler was installed as chancellor, things were different. While the home had earlier been tax exempt as a welfare institution, from 1933 this status no longer applied. Officials demanded a very high tax and required us to pay this tax retroactively for several of the past years.

From 1935 to 1937 we paid RM 20,000 annually, in six monthly installments.[7] From the year 1939, a further 50 percent retroactive tax was added to the above figure. Along with these heavy burdens, certain departments of the National Socialist government began interfering in the home's management.

HIGH POINT FOR THE HOME

In the meantime a beautiful celebration was held at the home on January 31, 1937, honoring my seventieth birthday. A friend who was present wrote to me a while ago: "As I recall the beautiful celebration two years ago, I am moved with uplifting but wistful memories. One can now maintain that this day represented the high point in our home for the elderly."

New burdens were constantly being added. Most of our occupants were dependent on family members to pay their fees, and the ability of these relatives to provide was constantly declining. Since we could never consider turning our occupants onto the street, the weight of our debts was increased by the inability of many occupants and their relatives to pay their fees.

About this time many young men and women were leaving the country and were pressed to find lodging for parents remaining behind. We began receiving a deluge of requests for residence as a result of political conditions. What could have been dearer to the hearts of these old-timers than to spend the rest of their days in the home for the elderly? But the home lacked the space to receive them!

---

7. This amount was equivalent to about $5,000, which is worth approximately $69,000 in terms of today's purchasing power.

In 1938 the home had to be expanded. By then there were always difficulties. In order to buy, build, or rent property for an annex, the administration had to approach government authorities who were no longer fully supportive as they once were. Certain departments of the National Socialist government were also interfering in our operations.

We thought of renting or buying a facility either in Neustadt or in another town of the Pfalz. An offer was made to sell us the Rosenstein Villa in Speyer with its spacious surrounding garden property for the price of RM 37,500. The estate was a completely enclosed piece of property with no neighbors on adjoining lots and plenty of space to expand at any time. A conditional purchase agreement was signed and notarized with a clause stating that its validity would depend on permission being granted by the city. After much indecision on the part of the authorities we were told an authorization to purchase would not be granted due to "strategic considerations." So the purchase became invalid.

While these negotiations were in progress, members of the committee also looked into other possibilities. They considered purchasing or renting the estate of the Rosenstiel brothers in Neustadt, where a winery retail-sales outlet had been operated until recently. We were willing to undertake extensive renovations and repairs, but in the end we were prevented from buying the Rosenstiel estate as well.

About this time the Neustadt city administration granted us permission to construct a new building on property adjoining our own. Plans were procured, but the building was never constructed due to problems with the authorities.

By that time, one injustice against the Jews followed close on the heels of the last. We began considering purchasing the estate on property adjoining our own, but within a short time the property was sold to a high school teacher instead. Since the proceeds of that purchase were no more than RM 35,000, the heir to the property received nothing from the deal. The administration of our home was then required to pay this party RM 1,500 out of our own funds to compensate him for his "loss"! Such was the unjust manner in which the National Socialist government interfered with our affairs.

As for plans for enlarging the home itself, a permit was eventually granted by the authorities of Neustadt, but, again, construction had to be postponed in favor of "more urgent building needs elsewhere."

The need for more space became desperate. A number of newcomers had to be housed and that was that! We succeeded in renting property for a two-year period and complied with the demand to pay the entire rental sum of RM 8,000 up front. After weeks of work, the home then housed twenty newcomers, bringing the total of those we cared for up to seventy in all. Still, an additional fifty were still waiting!

"DISMISSAL" ON FALSE PREMISES

During the summer of 1938, on July 22, three members of our association received an unexpected summons. The Gestapo of Neustadt ordered them to appear at a hearing that same afternoon and report to Mr. Wy, the informant for the state police on matters concerning Jews of the Pfalz. No explanation was given.

Mr. Wy, in his turn, had earlier relied heavily on a teacher, Mr. Sigmund Marx of Speyer, as his informer. Mr. Marx's primary responsibility had been to report on the mood of the Jewish people after they were summoned for their capital levy (a tax based on all capital holdings).

Mr. Wy had represented the authorities at our board meeting for the home earlier that day. At the meeting he showed surprise that Mr. Marx was not there. It was explained that Mr. Marx was neither interested in being part of our welfare institution, nor was he a member of the board.

THE HEARING

At the hearing Mr. Wy stated:

> "We Germans are living in a new time. The Jews must fit into the new conditions, and the leadership of the home for the elderly has to be concerned because you have been operating on a Zionist basis.
>
> For this reason and because of his advanced age, the president, Mr. Emil Behr, will have to step down. The teacher, Mr. Sigmund Marx of Speyer, will replace him. The other two men [in leadership posts] may retain their positions and make further appointments as they see fit. They will also be expected to report today's discussion to all members of the association in a newsletter or an advertisement in the local paper of the Pfalz."

The seventeen members of the board were then called to a special meeting on Sunday, July 31. Mr. Wy and the new president, Mr. Marx, were also present, representing the Gestapo. Mr. Behr had been required to step down and after that day never entered the home again.

On the agenda for the meeting was a resolution to reorganize the board. Another man, Dr. Karl Strauss, presided in the absence of Mr. Behr. He opened the meeting at the appointed time and, in a pathetically feeble voice, reported that three board members were told Mr. Behr must step down. He would "have to retire because of his age." He then told them a teacher, Mr. Sigmund Marx from Speyer, had been "suggested" as his replacement. This man, they had said, would be suitable as he was "close to the Zionist movement."

A feeling of heaviness pervaded the air. Our spirits were greatly dampened and no one requested the floor. Finally, Mr. Wy rose to speak, this time with conciliatory words:

> "Due to present conditions in the Pfalz, the Jews are especially hard hit. Though they have submitted to the situation, the only path that remains open to them is to emigrate. It is the responsibility of the home to accept such older persons whose children want to emigrate so as to help expedite the emigration of the younger generation. The authorities must see to it that the post of primary importance in the home will be held as long as possible by a man close to the Zionist movement. He should be a man devoted to the movement and one who earns the respect of those he works with. He will also need all of your support in order to… enlarge the home."

Thereafter Mr. Wy read a letter from Mr. Marx. In the letter Mr. Marx asked that Mr. Behr be reinstated and reappointed to the board, in view of his excellent accomplishments.

After the reading, this exchange followed:

Mr. Marx: "The sole intent of my letter, Mr. Wy, was to make my views on the situation known to the Gestapo.
"I have struggled much with this matter. The most difficult part is that I am required to drive a man from

his post who has identified with the work of the home with heart and soul."

Mr. Wy: "It will not be possible to comply with your request, Mr. Marx. It is not permissible to criticize the Gestapo. You will be obliged to accept the post of presidency!"

Mr. Marx: "In any event I will surely let Mr. Behr know of my personal appreciation for the unselfish way he has served the home."

I RESIGN

Mr. Marx then left his previous position, working with the young students at a school, to take on the presidency of our home. He had never been inclined to work with the elderly, but the state police had their eyes on him. He could no longer oppose their will.

His words to the board:

> "Although this position has been thrust on me, I desire nothing better than that the Lord will let me enjoy the trust of all participants. I will strive to carry out my tasks well so that when I later leave this post my highest reward will be the knowledge that I have done my duty.
>
> "Now I will be helping the elderly so as to pave the way for the young people. I hope also to continue working with the youth in some capacity.
>
> "Care for the elderly is one of the commandments. God's blessing will be upon those who abide by it. The home for the elderly bears witness to this truth. I urge you all to stand behind me and show me your support!"

In my case, having heard the words of Mr. Wy, I took the opportunity to submit my resignation. Hadn't he said, after all, that "the only path now open to Jews" was to leave the country?

I would immigrate to America. As treasurer for the home I assured him I had been attending to my duties in this honorable position since the home's founding over twenty-five years earlier. I was a single man with two children in America. Both my sons had urged me at length to come and live with them. I had always declined. I could refuse no longer. I would prepare for my departure after the books would be closed at year's end (1938).

I suggested that a suitable replacement would be Mr Albert Muelhauser of Speyer. Mr. Muelhauser had handled repeated audits of the books and had insight into the extent of the task, so the transition would not cause a gap in operations. There would be additional opportunity for Mr. Muelhauser to familiarize himself with the work before the end of the year.

My recommended replacement met with the agreement of all, Mr. Muelhauser included. Mr. Wy accepted these arrangements and the matter was settled. The board meeting closed with due formality. Sadly, it became the last of its kind before the home met its tragic demise.

TACTICS OF THE OVERLORDS

No sooner had that meeting closed than Mr. Wy instructed the journalist present, right in the presence of Mr. Marx, about how he should report the meeting to the Jewish community paper of the Pfalz. He was to state that Mr. Behr had stepped down *"of his own free will,* because of his age." He was not to indicate that he had been removed by the Gestapo. He was to say that Mr. Sigmund Marx had been unanimously elected to the presidency. A copy of his report was to be given to the Gestapo prior to printing.

I sought to intervene and prevent this, but it was no use. The matter was reported as Mr. Wy had demanded, giving a distorted picture of what had happened. Many reports in the German papers had been altered in the same way since the onset of the Hitler regime. Such were the unconscionable tactics of our Nazi overlords!

About the fate of Mr. Marx, he did not retain his position long as the Gestapo choice for president of our home. He was sent as a delegate from the Pfalz to a conference for the Jewish Union in Zurich, in the summer of 1939, and never returned. He went from there to France and ended up in a concentration camp.

Our joyous cornerstone-laying ceremony had taken place with pomp and dignity on September 29, 1912. The home for the Jewish elderly burned to the ground on Kristallnacht. In the interval everything had changed. The tenth of November 1938 became a day of sorrow for the Jews of Germany like so many days during the thousand-year history of our people.

I often thought of my son George as an alarmist. In the twenties and early thirties I was perfectly confident of my security as a loyal German citizen. Yet already in the early twenties, George made his decision to leave the town where he grew up for a new life across the sea. He saw nothing but dark clouds on Germany's horizon.

He wrote in his journal:

> The country has just lost a bloody war. Inflation has robbed the citizens of their last penny. The thought

of revenge for the shameful defeat of the Fatherland is slumbering in the mind of every German youth. For us in Speyer, which is situated near the long-contested border with France, another war seems unavoidable.

My son described how in 1923, when he left Germany, tension against the French military occupation in Speyer was building up. By then the bridge connecting Speyer with the west bank of the Rhine was no longer in use, closed by order of the French occupying forces.

> Feelings against the French have been running high in recent months. The townspeople are weary of the occupation. Five years since 1918, the end of the war, ought to be enough! But there is no end in sight! They resent the fraternizing of dark-skinned French troops with Speyer's female population. They object to severe disciplinary actions by the French authorities. The whole population suffers from the excesses of a handful of people.
>
> Most of the townspeople are known for their integrity. Yet if one drinks a toast in honor of the king's birthday or if a high school boy is caught whistling a patriotic song or a military march, he is sent to jail.
>
> The people resent the luxuries of the French officers, who have taken over the few good office buildings, club facilities, and "better homes" in town. They dislike their parades and military displays. Most of all our people object to French efforts to encourage a "separatist movement," pushing for

an independent Rhineland republic separate from Germany.

Two specific incidents have recently led to stern countermeasures by the French military. For almost any slight "misdemeanor" an upstanding citizen can suddenly be exiled from his home in Speyer. The story of one of Father's best friends, Mr. Bernhard Lang, is one such case.

Mr. Lang, like my father, was a teacher for over thirty years and now receives a government pension. He began assembling a group of former pupils who, like every German young man, yearned to sing patriotic songs and other traditional folk music. Once a week they met across the Rhine from Speyer in unoccupied Baden, where such singing was not *verboten*. They wanted to manifest their loyalty to the cause of German unity.

One of the few separatists in town heard of these "excesses" across the Rhine. Hoping for personal gain from the new masters, he succeeded in obtaining a photograph of the singing group for French authorities.

Mr. Lang was a levelheaded man, upright and law-abiding. He strictly avoided doing anything that could have been interpreted as subversive or directed against the French military. Yet that photo was enough to exile him from his beloved Speyer. He was forced to take refuge across the Rhine and later settled in Munich.

The second incident was far more serious. A group of young Germans, mostly Prussians, banded together into a secret organization in free

Germany, across the Rhine. They intended "to liberate Germany." They undoubtedly formed one of the early core groups from which the Nazi Party took form. Three or four of these youths crossed the Rhine from the Baden bank one day and made their way to the headquarters of the French occupying forces at Hotel Wittelsbacher Hof. They passed the armed sentries and shot the commanding officer.

As quickly as they had entered, they retreated to the Rhine and disappeared in a canoe. No one ever learned who they were. This caused a fury among the French military command. As a result many new restrictions and reprisals have been imposed on the population of Speyer. One of these is that all train and other traffic across the Rhine has been ordered suspended. The bridge, which was formerly opened only to let boat traffic pass through, has now been opened permanently.

UNFLAGGING PATRIOTISM

I personally expressed strong sentiments of patriotism both at home and in my teaching. My son, in fact, held that my love for my country was "boundless":

> Father's patriotism was...well-known among his colleagues. He loved Speyer. He loved Germany, the king, and the Kaiser probably more than any other teacher in town. Father's great ambition was that he and his sons should sacrifice everything for the beloved Fatherland should there be another war with France. He taught us that Germany was surrounded by jealous, hostile neighbors who might

find a pretext at any time for breaking the armistice and going to war with us.

George learned of various anti-Semitic incidents I contended with in my profession. I would never have told him or his brother about these happenings, not wanting to trouble their young minds. But the stories circulated and came back to their ears.

George told in his journal:

Among the gentile boys and girls Father is generally held in high esteem. Yet there are some who refrain from lifting their hats in courtesy when meeting him on the street. Once he could not keep from asking the neighbor boy whom he meets each morning walking to school:

"Son, don't you know me?"

"Yes, I know you," replied the boy. "You are Mr. Waldbott of our school. But my father told me never to take my hat off for a Jew. You crucified Christ."

Another case concerned one of the Protestant teachers at school, many of whom are among father's closest friends. Yet he has one colleague who makes life uncomfortable for him. This man probably has a chip on his shoulder. He feels somewhat of a failure in his own family, one of the German nobility. Other family members are either army officers or high government officials, and he is only a teacher. Such people sometimes try to compensate for their feelings of inferiority by putting on a superior air toward persons in a minority.

Whenever Father plays cards with the other teachers in the half-hour recess after lunch at Café Weibel, this man avoids him. He will not come near the table where Father sits.

In concluding this journal entry I want to credit my father concerning a great gift that he has. He manages to quickly overlook any rebuff or insult that comes his way and can hastily dismiss an unwelcome incident from his mind.

CHAPTER FOUR

Desecration and Boyhood Passions

It was not only in connection with my teaching that I, Leo, witnessed heartless acts of anti Semitism. I recall one occasion when George as a small boy was with me. We were on one of our regular pilgrimages to the little village of Weingarden. When we arrived he was confronted with the desecration of his grandfather's grave and was shocked at what he saw:

> Each fall, in early October, Father and I visited my paternal grandfather's grave, where we cleared away the weeds, said a prayer, and laid a pebble on the gravestone in reverence to the deceased. This pebble also served as a sign that we'd been there.
>
> We boarded the one-track train in Speyer, nicknamed the "peppermint track" by the boys at home. Its pathway was flanked with peppermint greenery and the scent permeated the air. The train took us past beautiful pine forests and sand hills where asparagus was raised, then chugged along in the direction of the vineyards near Neustadt.

After disembarking at the village station, we had a good hour's hike to reach the graveyard. On these hikes we would marvel at the beauty of the fall colors of maples and oaks, then at their height Their bright red hues alternated with the greens of the apple trees. The sweet, minty fragrance from the dense foliage gave a certain character to this whole area that I have never seen elsewhere.

When we would reach the cemetery, we never saw a soul except on one occasion. This time a well-dressed, older gentleman was busying himself with some of the gravestones. He was evidently there for the same purpose as we were. A few feet away a hazel-eyed girl in a red dress and white pinafore, slightly younger than me, was kneeling down by a grave and seemed to be picking flowers. As we drew closer I could see she was actually scraping something off the gravestone with a rock.

"Have they desecrated our stones again?" Father asked the old man.

He nodded with a pained expression.

More than half of the stones were covered with vile and sordid words. Two gravestones had been thrown off their sockets and smashed to pieces.

We notified the police, and two gendarmes came out to investigate. They inspected the graveyard with the thoroughness and competency of a German bureaucrat and took careful notes. Then they quickly assured us there was nothing to be done. They could never find the culprits!

Father was saddened by what he had seen. It seemed impossible to him that adult Germans could have committed such savagery.

"Don't you think they must have been just a few wild boys?" he asked the old man.

"Perhaps, but this is very doubtful, sir. There is a rumor in our village that this is the deed of an organized gang with adults as leaders."

I felt entirely different about it. I shuddered at the thought that such an outrage could have been committed by the same kind of Germans who were my neighbors, the so-called friends of my father and the boys who sat beside me in class.

For the first time in my life I began to wonder where I stood in German society. I was confused. Indeed, I was frightened.

"Toni, My Eldest"

The girl must have observed my concern. Her pretty brown eyes looked directly at me. She had stopped her work of cleaning the old gravestone.

"It isn't so serious, sir. Anti-Semitism is much worse in our village than elsewhere in this area, but it soon blows over in small villages like ours."

She must have been aware that we came from Speyer. We dressed like city people, and Speyer was the only city from which the train could have brought us.

I was amazed that she had given this matter such thought and seemed to have a definite opinion about it.

"I certainly do hope so, Fraulein," I replied gravely. "It is a bad thing."

In the meantime Father had walked over to his father's grave and was inspecting the hammer blows on the inscription.

"Have they damaged your gravestone, too?" the old man asked. Then his eyes fell on the inscription.

"Oh, you must be Mr. Waldbott from Speyer. Isn't this exciting! My name is Furst, Isaac Furst of Weingarten. I am doubly glad to make your acquaintance as you will soon be the teacher of my girls."

"How is this possible?" Father replied, startled.

"This is Toni, my eldest. We will be moving to Speyer about Christmas."

"What a coincidence! I'm pleased to meet you. I've already been told the congregation will soon be having a new member from your village. May I introduce my son George?"

I took off my hat and, in good German fashion, bent low at the waist and clicked my heels together.

"We are forced to move away from this pretty spot which we all love, unfortunately. Our two girls were born and raised here. Yet we're moving for their sake. The *Burgemeister* hates us."

"How on earth can this be?" Father responded with alarm.

"You see, he, too, is an insurance salesman. He's my only competitor in this district. His best stock in

Desecration and Boyhood Passions

trade is to propagate rumors among his prospects that Jews are dishonest and swindle people out of their money.

"It all dates back to the time he lost a good life insurance sale to me. People have told me he lost the prospect because he had been drunk for a whole week. He blamed me for it and tried to ruin my good name. Yes, I did sell the insurance, but I offered half the commission to the Burgermeister. In spite of this he called me a dirty crook and a filthy Jew or some such usual byword referring to my religion."

I was listening to his story with open mouth. I even forgot for a moment that I was in the presence of one of the most charming girls I'd ever met. This was my first real encounter with anti-Semitism. If a man was incompetent and wanted to knock out his Jewish competitor he could resort to Jew-baiting. This is what had happened. Now Mr. Furst was leaving the insurance field in that region, all because of a drunkard!

We stood staring silently at the desecrated graves. Suddenly Father rose and stood upright.

"I don't believe this, sir. It sounds impossible," he exclaimed.

He could not deal with a tale that showed his German compatriots in such miserable light.

Mr. Gan's Dry-Goods Shop
The old man responded calmly by relating another incident from his village.

"There is no more honest and trustworthy person in Weingarten than Mr. Gans, owner of the little dry-goods shop. His family has owned it and has been living above the shop for over two hundred years. They ruined his business, too. His competitor, Steinhauser, started a whispering campaign, spreading a tale that Gans's mother had immigrated from Russia."

It was common knowledge at that time among German Jews that an eastern Jew was considered to be like the devil himself. No good German could trust him.

"Now Mr. Gans wants to move away but he doesn't know where to go. Haven't you heard such stories before, Mr. Waldbott? Things must be much better in a larger town like yours."

Father didn't answer. He would certainly not believe anything that would incriminate a German without more evidence than Mr. Furst's word. As for myself, I couldn't offer any answer either. I was totally perplexed by these stories, as the ugly face of anti-Semitism had never showed itself openly to me before. I simply wasn't aware of such things.

Beautiful Toni

I felt deeply concerned and dejected by all this. At the same time, there was something mysterious stirring within me. I felt jubilant in spite of everything. It was the presence of Toni. I could hardly take my eyes off her. Her full braids hanging down her back blended with the orange tones of her jacket. Every so often she glanced shyly toward me, and each time I would try furtively to catch her eye, if for only a second.

Desecration and Boyhood Passions

I was eager to start a conversation. But dare I talk to her? It would have been unheard for me to talk to a girl in Father's presence. And what would she think if I were to address her first? Did I lack the courage to start a conversation? I couldn't bear that thought. I wasn't a coward. So I walked over to where she stood and was just about to tell her how well she had cleaned up the gravestone when her father interrupted the silence.

"Would you like to take a hike over to our home for a glass of beer and some homemade cheese? We could be there in a few minutes."

How I wanted to be near beautiful Toni a little longer.

It would have only been a short hike. Yet somehow I hoped Father would not accept. Something drew me away from this beautiful scenery with the quaint old houses surrounded by vineyards and separated from the meadows by a meandering brook and even from lovely Toni. It was the drunk Burgemeister, Mr. Steinhauser the merchant, the two gendarmes who were not interested in catching the culprits. It was the gang that desecrated the graves. It was the ugly face of anti-Semitism perched right above the church steeple. Father must have felt the same way.

"We have to figure on a whole hour to reach the station. We should leave here very soon. If we don't, we won't make the afternoon train," Father insisted.

Looking back now, I, Leo, have to acknowledge that the desecration of our cemeteries became increasingly common as time went on, particularly during the presidency of Marshall von Hindenburg (1925–27). According to Marvin Lowenthal in his book *The Jews of Germany* (1938), under Hindenburg, racist parties steadily grew stronger and more influential. He noted that, just as we had experienced that day, "The perpetrators of outrages against cemeteries and synagogues usually managed to elude the arm of justice."

In those days I condoned everything the Germans did, no matter how wrong toward me and my people. Today I ask questions. Why are the Jews the ones always subjected to savagery and humiliation? What have we done to deserve it? Nobody asks to be born a Jew. The choice is not ours.

The Jewish writer Sholem Asch addresses this question in his book *The Apostle*. The key character shows that Jewish persecution throughout the ages is a two-sided coin. On the one side "Israel is as a worm under the feet of the nations." And on the other, "Israel is the star of mankind... and the pillar of fire which goes before the whole world on the path of redemption."

A TWOFOLD AWAKENING

It was years later that George shared with me what he had written in his journal after the hike home from the cemetery. During that trek his mind had been under fire from two angles. A new awareness of bad feelings toward our people and his boyhood love passions had been simultaneously awakened:

> Toni and her father were disappointed we would not join them for refreshments:
> "This is too bad," our companions responded simultaneously.

"It's very kind of you to invite us and we shall certainly get together in Speyer once you're settled," Father assured them.

This latter remark kept my mind occupied the whole trip home. Would I see Toni again? Perhaps they would come and visit or we might visit them. On the way to the station we filled our pockets with apples lying everywhere on the path. I strolled behind Father so that he could not watch me picking daisies and pulling off the petals. I simply had to know whether she loved me or not.

For some reason the response of the daisies was unkind and always gave the wrong answer. But I wasn't downcast! I knew better. She had given me one direct glance, looking straight into my eyes. That glance meant more than the daisy petals!

But had I failed to respond as I should? Shouldn't I have given her some sign of how I felt? Would she know I liked her?

This worried me. I had not made the best of my chances.

Then again, anti-Semitism! This wasn't directed only against Mr. Gans and Mr. Furst. It concerned me personally. Was I to grow up and live among people who didn't consider me one of them and who failed to punish those who committed unjust deeds against me? Wouldn't it be best to move far, far away? If need be, to the North Pole, to Central America, or Asia, where presumably no one could hurt me.

Father was still walking ahead of me. To him the whole matter was trivial. I could not discuss it with him. The Germans could do no wrong. And to talk to him about Toni was impossible. He might have punished me for letting a silly love distract me from important things like my studies.

I kept on walking with my eyes on the daisies, the peppermint plants, and the apples lying on the road.

This was just one story of my son's weakness for the opposite sex. There were others. He has also recently shared an excerpt from his journal concerning our neighbor, Paula Bender, who never became more than a neighbor either but whom George found most attractive:

As a boy growing up a lovely girl always caught my eye – not the girls with the painted faces we often see today but those with the natural beauty that shines from within.

Paula Bender was such a girl. She was dark-eyed, about my age, and had two long braids flowing down her back. Some mornings I had the thrill of catching sight of her from our front room as she stepped outside, closed the door of her home behind her, and walked straight toward my window. I would try to make the most of my opportunity by sitting down at the piano and performing the most delightful Chopin waltz just as she passed.

A few times I caught her eye as she glanced up. Once she must have especially enjoyed the music, because before turning the corner she slowed down and stood still for a few seconds. Not wanting to let on what she may have been feeling, she fastened her eyes on the ground as though searching for a lost coin. Since then whenever I play this part of that particular Chopin waltz I think of the coin Paula Bender might or might not have lost. I never had the chance to speak to her, but I noted many times how she sent longing glances toward my window.

CHAPTER FIVE

My Sons Depart

My older son, Emil, was the first to leave home to begin a new life across the sea. This was in 1910, when he was a young man of nineteen. He saw opportunities for himself in the cigar industry and was eager to try his hand at doing business in the "New World." As things worked out, after his marriage to Helen Ullman, he settled for a partnership with his brother-in-law in the ownership and management of a soft-drink company.

In 1923 my younger son, George, also departed from home to establish himself as a doctor in America.

George described his departure at length in his journal, which began with the crossing of the Rhine in a small skiff and with an emotional battle in saying farewell:

> June 1923
>
> The rays of the rising sun shone across the Rhine River, breaking on the little rowboat heading into the waves from the left bank near the venerable city of Speyer. The boat's owner, Seppel Schreiner, was a young man accustomed to negotiating this crossing in his small skiff. Ever since the bridge had been

ordered closed by the French, he had been transporting passengers daily, one or two per crossing, into the unoccupied, free zone of post-World War I Germany. Seppel's powerful arms dexterously manipulated the oars, skirting the whirlpools, and navigated through the strong current with the skill of one who could deal with the treacherous waves.

I was sitting on a suitcase, which held all my worldly things. In my hand was a handkerchief that I was solemnly waving toward a white-haired gentleman standing motionless on the shore. Two young girls stood beside him, also waving incessantly. These were two cousins who had made the trip to Speyer from nearby Ruchheim to bid me farewell.

But the elderly man, my father, simply stood motionless, clutching his handkerchief in one hand and using it to repeatedly wipe away the tears coursing down his cheeks – tears that had been dampening his face from the moment we left home to walk down to the river.

As the little boat pulled away from the shore, a gentle breeze wafted fragrant scents toward us from the rows of blossoming chestnut trees, willows, and poplars flanking the shore. But this day I paid little attention. I failed also to observe the gradually expanding silhouette of the old town with its quaint houses and towers and church steeples. I was even blind to the magnificent Romanesque cathedral, the focal point of the city – the Kaiserdom with its huge cupola rising majestically from behind those three figures standing on the shore.

My thoughts were only with my father. I would not see him again for a long time. No one knew how long.

The Risk-Laden Rhine

Seppel pulled hard on the oars as we reached a precarious juncture in the river where the stream swerved sharply and the waves rose two to three feet high. The current was strong there, and the small rowboat was shoved off course and carried rapidly downstream.

This risk-laden bend in the river was well-known to every boy in Speyer. Swimmers had to avoid it at all costs. On unpropitious occasions youngsters bathing in the vicinity had been caught up in the powerful current and carried midstream. Unless they were strong swimmers they would give up the struggle to reach the opposite shore of the mile-wide river and perish in the turbulent waters.

My eyes remained focused on that one point on the shore. Still waving my kerchief like a white flag of surrender, I failed even to notice that Seppel was rowing now with less effort. We were in calmer waters again. Amidst the monotonous creaking of the oars and lapping of the waves against the starboard of the skiff, Seppel looked up from his steady movements and caught my eye.

"Herr Doktor, couldn't you reconsider? Don't you think you can change your mind?"

I was startled by his question. I didn't even grasp it at first.

"Just think of your poor father. His first son left him ten years ago for America. His only daughter died. His good wife lies in the grave. You are the last one he has. You should not be leaving him like this. Couldn't you stay and open an office in Speyer?"

A Knot in My Throat
Something was gripping my throat. I couldn't answer. My handkerchief was still fluttering in the wind.

Ever since I was a small boy dreaming of becoming a doctor I had seen myself with a large medical office in a prosperous residence in my hometown of Speyer. But things had changed. For a number of years I had been pondering over my future and that of my home and my father. The matter of greatest concern was the future of my country. As I looked coldly at the current political and social conditions, I saw nothing but dark clouds ahead for Germany. German youth burned with a desire for revenge against France for Germany's shameful defeat in World War 1. The handwriting was on the wall. Another war seemed inevitable.

As for my personal prospects, there were already too many doctors in Speyer. It would be difficult to make a living there. I had concluded that there was no future for me in Speyer or anywhere in Germany. I felt driven to leave my country and my dear father, as well.

Prospects seemed rosy for me in America. I had a good job waiting. I would be the assistant to Dr. Hugo Freund, the best-known diagnostician

My Sons Depart

in Detroit, where I was headed. My mother's sister also lived in Detroit. She was a marvelous person whom I knew would be like a mother to me. My brother, too, would be there to help me. I had everything to gain.

My plan was fine except for the matter about which Seppel felt so strongly. In leaving Father alone in the "Old World" I seemed to be deserting him. We had had long discussions, Father and I. My father was broad-minded and generous. He insisted that I not change my plans for his sake only. I, for my part, resolved to see Father either in the United States or in Germany, once a year. In addition, as soon as I had a firm foothold in the United States, I would arrange for him to follow me, my brother, and other relatives who had already immigrated to the New World.

Finally, the tight knot eased somewhat and I replied to Seppel's question:

"I can't help it. There is no other choice for me. We can't always do what we want in this world. Father helped me make up my mind."

Seppel sighed deeply and buried his head deep in his lap. He kept pulling on his oars. After a moment's silence he commented, "Yes, you are right. Your father will get over it. He has many good friends who will cheer him up between your visits."

The boat was now in calmer waters heading into the Old Rhine. It was no secret that the damming of the river and other measures of flood control such as the building of tree-lined pumping stations had been the work of Napoleon I, over a hundred years earlier.

Dating from the time Napoleon's forces occupied this territory, numerous major improvements had been made, those which contributed to the smooth flow of the river and others that concerned better road conditions – improvements from which the occupied German population drew benefit and took some comfort. Yet everyone knew these improvements were intended primarily to serve Napoleon's own goals. The roads and dikes were improved and put in place for the security of Napoleon's armies.

The Old Pontoon Bridge

The steady movement of Seppel's powerful arms was bringing us upstream toward the old pontoon bridge that connected Speyer with the right bank – a bridge that belonged to the German state of Baden. Rows of willows and poplars alternating with the many lagoons caused us to gradually lose sight of my father and the two girls still waving on the shore.

But why this unusual and cumbersome mode of travel? Because all traffic across the Rhine had been discontinued as a penal measure against the townspeople by the French occupation forces. In order to make the crossing now, travel by small boat was the only option.

How different it had been when we were boys. We would often walk across the bridge on foot or ride across the Rhine in one of Mr. Seydal's horse-drawn carriages, the taxis of the day.

My Sons Depart

Watching trains cross the pontoon bridge had been a visual experience for young and old alike. First to cross would be the heavy locomotive and behind it came one train car after another, each weighing down the pontoon on which it was being carried and causing it to sink deep into the river. We watched as the pontoons would gradually rise again as the lighter cars brought up the rear and began crossing. And finally the caboose! The whole procession resembled a huge caterpillar in action as it crept forward.

In the center of the river three sections of the four pontoons that made up the bridge could be unlinked whenever a ship or barge approached. For the people of Speyer it was a favorite pastime to stand watching the boats pass through the bridge.

The bearded and aging bridge master would first haul down the blue-and-white Bavarian flag, replacing it with a red one to signal that oncoming traffic must come to a halt. This included vehicles such as hay wagons, oxcarts, and fiacres. Then the clanging of a bell would summon the bridge personnel to their stations. There would be a rattling and unwinding of the chains that anchored each section upstream and a rumbling of the ropes, so boards and links between the sections could be removed. Then the unlinked parts of the bridge were opened and pushed aside with ropes and poles. Finally, we onlookers watched eagerly as the vessels steamed by, often with five or six heavily loaded barges trailing behind. But nothing of this took place anymore since the bridge was open permanently.

As Seppel's small rowboat drew closer to the bridge, he pointed out the provisional railroad station where my long trip would begin. In the distance we could see the Lusshof, where Mr. Lang used to assemble his boys in free Germany for sessions of singing and loyally hailing the Fatherland – sessions which were abruptly ended the day their project became known to the French.

Seppel's Gift
Seppel stopped rowing and looked at me curiously. He seemed to have something to say but couldn't get it out. Then he finally found the words:

> "Mother and I were talking about you this morning on the way to mass. 'Seppel,' she said, 'Don't take a *pfennig* [a German penny] from him for this trip. I never had a chance to repay his mother – God bless her soul! – for what she did for me.'
> "Did she ever tell you?"
> "I don't know. She never talked much about the good things she did."
> "Way back in 1917, when you and I were in the service and everyone was short of food, Mother was carrying my little sister. She was very ill and old Dr. Rice told Father she might not pull through. For weeks your mother used to come every morning and give Mother a part of her quota of milk. Once she even brought a bowl of chicken soup."

My Sons Depart

All this time Seppel had had his hand in his pocket holding something that seemed precious to him.

"She said I should give this to you. She had it blessed this morning by the priest in the Kaiserdom, and I know it will bring you luck." He hesitated. "I know it is against your religion to carry a cross with you but you must take it."

The thought of my mother brought tears to my eyes. Father was well acquainted with everyone in town but I had no idea that Seppel and his mother had known my mother. His reference to my religion startled me for a moment. Indeed, some of the Orthodox members of the 120 Jewish families in town would have considered it a blasphemy for Mr. Waldbott's son to accept a cross.

Nonetheless, I leaned over in the boat, reached for the little cross, and buried it in my wallet.

"Thank you, Seppel. I shall always carry it in my wallet and think of your mother and mine."

A few more strokes of the oars and we reached the rocks from where a path lead through the willow trees toward the base of the bridge. I grabbed my suitcase, jumped out of the boat, and hurried on my way.

Nearly an hour remained before the train's departure, so I selected a little spot on the grass from which I could clearly view the river and the towers of the old city on the opposite shore. Most of the twenty-five years of my life were part and parcel with this town that I was leaving for good. True, I had been "out in the world" during my student days and in the Army. Yet the character, the habits, the thinking and the actions of everyone who grew up here, myself included, seemed fashioned into a certain mold typical of the people of Speyer.

It was some years later when I heard about the little cross George received from Seppel. Frankly, the thought distressed me. Yet I comforted myself by remembering that Seppel and his mother had given it to my son not out of ill will but as a token of his mother's appreciation for my wife's selfless and loving deed. Their intent had been harmless.

THE TOWN LEFT BEHIND

George had torn himself away physically from the country and town he loved – and for good reason as things turned out. Yet my son, now established with his medical practice in America, reminisces nostalgically about the town still in his heart. He describes the distinctive features of Speyer that stood out in marked contrast to modern cities, most of which are laid out in a more or less uniform fashion:

> The town of Speyer is an ancient Kaiserstadt, a seat of past German emperors. Part of the medieval walls of the old city still stand, and beneath the majestic old Kaiserdom, eight German emperors lay buried.
>
> The main entrance to central Speyer, the *Alt Portel*, or High Gate, is one of three ancient landmarks. The other two are the magnificent old dome and the newer Gothic cathedral – also an impressive structure built in commemoration of the Diet

My Sons Depart

of Speyer, the general assembly of the Holy Roman Empire, where Martin Luther protested against the Catholic church in 1526. These three landmarks give a highly individualistic character to the town. Speyer stood out in marked contrast to modern-day Western cities laid out in a more or less uniform pattern.

When I was a child, the street connecting the dome and the Alt Portel was Hauptstrasse, or Main Street, where most business and cultural life in the town were conducted. It was a fairly straight and wide thoroughfare unlike other roads dating back at least six to eight centuries.

In most of the buildings families would combine their home and business in one residence. Often the same family had lived and labored in the same dwelling, generation after generation, for hundreds of years. There was Sauer's grocery, Ebert's pastry shop, Stoye's apothecary, Café Weibel, and the Steinhauser butcher shop. Undoubtedly, a person who visits Speyer a hundred years from now will still find a Mr. Sauer proudly displaying his delicious imported and domestic groceries, a Mr. Ebert still making pastries as exquisite as those he makes now, and a Mr. Stoye dispensing his drugs as conscientiously as the Mr. Stoye of today.

The name of the street, however, has undergone many changes during a period of thirty years. When I was born in 1898, it was Maximilian Street, in honor of the wise and popular King of Bavaria, Maximilian I. After 1918 and the abdication of the king, it assumed the name of Germany's first president as Ebertstrasse. After 1932, like other main streets in Germany, it became Adolf Hitler Strasse.[8]

---

8. Finally, when the self-styled "great benefactor" of Germany was no longer alive, the former name of Ebertstrasse was restored to signs at the intersections.

CHAPTER SIX

Mocking Caricatures and "Racial Disgrace"

In 1934, toward the end of October, my son George and his family came from America to visit me. As he understood that Hitler was, step by step, tightening the reins on the Jewish population, he knew this would be his last chance to see me in the beloved homeland. He was also interested in viewing firsthand the growing conditions of oppression for our people and to do what he could to rescue one or two.

George again kept a diary during that trip from which I will quote a few entries, revealing the worsening conditions in Germany at that time:

> October 24 – On board *The Bremen* we met a man, Mr. Nonius from Ludwigshafen, who had been in the United States conducting some business with Ford Motor Company in Detroit and was now returning to Germany. As we began speaking about the Jewish question, Mr. Nonius commented: "I cannot understand how the Jewish people were able to provoke the World War [World War 1]." When I asked him how he could imagine such a thing, he replied that he had no idea how they had carried this

CRYSTAL FRAGMENTS

out, but he knew it was "an established fact." People are hypnotized by the propaganda.

October 28 – Upon our arrival in Bremen what we saw seemed to be a complete militarization. All men were in uniform. The whole of Germany seemed to be a great military camp.

October 31 – In front of the theater in Heidelberg we observed the following sign: "Rothschild's Victory at Waterloo," an obvious expression of anti-Semitic propaganda.

November 4 – When passing through the village of Schwegenheim we were shocked by a sign at a gas station displaying the enlarged faces of men with typical Jewish features, and underneath these faces were these words: "These criminals are our misfortune." On another sign we read: "Drive 10 kilometers/hour! Jews drive 100 kilometers/hour!"

November 5 – At a building site on a new street in Frankenstein we read this sign: "Here our Führer gave bread and work to 200 fellow Germans. We will be true to our Führer until death."

November 6 – At the University of Heidelberg the famous professors Krehl, Willman, and Bethmann had been replaced by Nazis in good standing who, nonetheless, had no reputation as scientists. Professor Moro still remained in the children's clinic but was noticeably depressed and insistently refused to discuss political issues. Whenever students or nurses walked past they always raised their hands with the "Heil Hitler!" greeting.

November 8 – Mrs. Willy Mayer tells us that she has been asked to make a contribution to public welfare even though she is Jewish.

November 9 – Today is Memorial Day commemorating the National Socialist revolution. Flags are flying everywhere, but Jews are not allowed to fly any flags.

November 12 – Dr. Mandelbaum of Munich (previously a professor at the Schwabinger Hospital), who holds the Pettenkofer Prize, well-deserved for his service in southern Bavaria in the fight against typhus and diphtheria, tells me he has lost his job. In its place he now receives a pension amounting to RM 600. He had intended to set up a lab in his own home in order to continue with his research, but this also was denied him.

November 13 – While we were eating lunch in a hotel, our car was parked on the street in front of the building. As we were leaving we saw two Christian people standing in front of the car. As it turned out, they had been waiting there for an hour. Though they were strangers to us, they requested that we send them each an affidavit from America enabling them to leave Germany, which they wished to do by any means whatsoever.

November 13 – As we drove through the Mittelfranken area we saw signs on houses in each small village and even the smallest suburbs that read: "Jews not wanted" or "Jews are our misfortune." In Nürnberg we saw many signs stating: "German doctor."

In Nürnberg we visited a friend, Dr. Leo Landenberger, a man often sought out in former times for counsel as an attorney and who is now serving in the Government Federation of the German Jews. His present task is to keep a close watch on the living conditions of the Jews. He informed us that there are only five Jewish lawyers in Nürnberg today as compared with some fifty practicing law before the time of Hitler. Two large Jewish firms in the city have closed. Jewish businessmen are in despair generally.

On public buildings one observes large billboards picturing a fox and inscribed with the words:

"Trust not a fox in a green meadow nor a Jew by his oath!"

The Jews in Nürnberg are completely isolated and in constant fear of being shipped off to a concentration camp. Every hotel and restaurant bears the sign "Jews not welcome." Dr. Landenberger gave us names of eight Jews who were deported to Dachau to be shot. Relating the case of a further atrocity, he told of a Jewish boy who was standing and talking on the street with a Christian neighbor, a young girl. He was apprehended by the ss and brought to Dachau. His ashes were sent to his parents a few days later. The charge against him is said to have been "racial disgrace."

In another case, a doctor was about to be released from the camp, however on the day before his release he received such a cruel beating that he later hanged himself.

After parting from Dr. Landenberger we drove to a castle where we were shown tools of martyrdom from the Middle Ages. This gave us cause for serious thought and troubled us so deeply we were obliged to cancel our plans to visit the beautiful city of Rothenburg on the Tauber.

November 19 – Speyer: A group of Hitler Youth are marching along and singing: "When the blood of Jews squirts from the tip of the knife, then it will be well with our land."

November 21 – In the region of the Saarland, along the route to Paris, just prior to elections, we observed the same signs in the windows of Jewish businessmen as those in windows of the Christians: "We vote for Germany." We spoke with some non-Jews who explained they displayed these signs out of fear of punishment in case the elections should result in a victory for the National Socialist Party.

November 30 – One of my non-Jewish school friends invited me to Kaiserslautern for a reunion. When the reunion took place three days later my friends were as friendly as ever. Each of them spoke out strongly against the anti-Jewish activities. Mr. Elkan visited me in my parents' home with one of his relatives. The latter told he had been one of the people hauled out of the synagogue and beaten in such a way that three of the men lay dead on the ground when the beating was over. Most of the others, himself included, had to be hospitalized for their injuries.

ONE LIFE SAVED

My son clearly perceived what was happening and decided while still in Germany to bring one Jewish girl with him to the United States. In our area no young girl was found willing to leave her parents and family home on such short notice. Many would later regret this.

There were cases a few years later, however, where families took advantage of my son's offer while there was still time. Greta Frank was one such a case. George had told her father that whenever she decided she wanted to come he would be willing to help her.

Greta, who was then twenty-three, arrived in the United States and proceeded to Michigan in January 1937. She lived with George and his family, helping care for the children for her first few months there, before finding work elsewhere. There were others who accepted his offer and lived with George and family in their tiny home on a busy street until they got their bearings in the new country.

In Nürnberg the picture was very different already as far back as 1934. Dr. Landenberger was told of my son's intentions, and two days later George received five letters from young women asking for help to leave Germany. A telegram was sent to only one. Miss Fl. was the young woman he chose, requesting her to come to Speyer so we could drive her from there to the American consulate in Stuttgart. She came at once, but in Stuttgart the American consulate was closed for the American Thanksgiving holiday. My son phoned the consul, nonetheless, with a great sense of urgency.

His response: "I would gladly perform the errand despite the holiday but no document would be valid in America if dated on Thanksgiving."

So we returned to Stuttgart again with Miss Fl. the following Monday. She was told she must meet us there at ten A.M. sharp and be ready to leave for America at once. She arrived on time with her father and this time received her visa two hours later. We spent the next day together in my home, and friends of my son exchanged many good wishes. Early the following morning, my son, his wife, and their two children together with Miss Fl. set off for Bremen. Though their return visit to the homeland had not been very enjoyable, they did have the pleasure of seeing his parents' home once more. Furthermore, my son was able to take nine volumes of his valuable stamp collection with him. The rest I brought him in 1936.

At that time we Jews, for the most part, didn't yet realize the seriousness of the situation. We viewed the grim circumstances as only temporary. There were many Jewish people

Mocking Caricatures and "Racial Disgrace"

who emigrated, nonetheless. These were the wakeful ones. By leaving Germany they escaped the difficulties which would escalate in coming years. At this time it was still possible to take along at least part of one's belongings and a certain amount of currency. All this would cease very shortly and emigrants would begin arriving at their destinations with only a few bags and two empty hands.

YOU CANNOT HAVE A PASSPORT!

I visited the United States seven times before December 1938. My wife was with me the first time, in 1909. The Regional Government of the Pfalz had kindly granted me an extra ten days of vacation, and this meant I was free to be away for about eight and a half weeks.

A significant episode occurred prior to my sixth trip in the spring of 1933, at the beginning of the Nazi regime. At the agency where I went to obtain my passport, the following exchange took place between the official and me:

"What is your religious confession?"

"I am a Jew."

"Then you cannot receive a passport."

"Is this your final decision or may I pursue my request at a higher level?"

The official then provided me with the name of an officer at the headquarters of the state police, whom I located after much difficulty. When I presented my request, mentioning the previous refusal, this man bluntly replied:

"The official did the right thing. We don't give passports to Jews. They only travel to foreign countries and promote anti-German propaganda."

Then I asked if I could tell him something about myself, and I told him:

"I have visited my children in America five times in the past. During my most recent trips when hatred against the Germans was on the rise due to World War I, I have always made a point of standing up for Germany and defending my fatherland. Furthermore, I want very much to return to Speyer in three months time and I know exactly what would happen to me if it were discovered that I had spread anti-German propaganda while abroad. Do you think I am so foolish that I haven't given this matter any thought?!"

"Well, come back in a week and you will receive your passport."

This I did and so was able to travel.

THE REUNIONS

It was always a great joy for all of us to meet at reunions of the Protestant Teachers' Seminary from which I graduated in 1885. At the time I entered the service of the public schools, sixty-five of my "Christian" colleagues did so as well. The bonds of friendship between us remained strong, and reunions were arranged after twenty-five, thirty, and forty years. In latter years this reunion took place annually in different towns of the Pfalz. One recognized the fidelity of a true friend by the way he shook your hand.

Each took a personal interest in the others' lives, their jobs, their family life, and so on. We would have rich exchanges of thoughts and experiences. The occasion was especially memorable when other family members would join us.

Then the year 1933 came along. I traveled to America in May of that year. When I was already in Bremen on my way, I received a letter from my colleague, Mr. Neumüller, who was in charge of practical arrangements for the reunion. He wrote that he would be delivering a special letter to me indicating the time and place for our gathering. This was a precaution he was taking because of the political situation. In his letter he criticized the actions of the government against the Jewish people in a very sensitive and thoughtful manner and assured me that none of our colleagues agreed with what was going on. He indicated that the close bonds of mutual love and trust that had held us together over many years would never diminish, and that I was expected at the reunion by all of the colleagues. I acknowledged his letter later on board ship and declined with a heavy heart.

Others years followed when I came in contact with this circle of friends, although I did not attend in 1936, as I traveled abroad.

Our subsequent meeting was held in Neustadt on the Haardt River in the conference hall of the Saalbau Hotel. When I got there, a number of colleagues had not yet arrived. Then our friend Philipp Fauth from Munich entered the hall. Philipp had become famous for his studies in astronomy. His name can be found today in every new encyclopedia. His accomplishments made him the pride of our group.

Passing by the other twenty-two colleagues, he walked straight up to me, greeting me with these words:

"You are the first person whose hand I want to shake!"

That was in 1937.

"DEAR EDOUARD, DON'T BE UPSET!"

On a beautiful spring day in 1938, my good friend and former class-mate from Speyer, Ed Mang, visited me in my home. He entered and addressed me with tears in his eyes:

"I have come with a very difficult task today. Our friend, Neumüller, didn't have the heart to say it to you in a letter."

He paused, cleared his throat:

"We greatly regret that we have to ask you to stay away from our next reunion."

Again a pause as he seemed to be choking on his words:

"As you know, our friends and their wives may bring their sons and daughters. Some of these young people hold public office and they fear participating in a gathering with a Jewish man would damage their image."

I cut my friend short, not letting him continue and I assured him:

"Dear Edouard, don't be upset about this. I have been expecting it for a long time, but I've held my peace. We Jews are used to such things. This will not damage our friendship."

Other painful events followed. For years I had belonged to a stamp collectors' club in Speyer composed of about fifty members. Of this number, I and one other member were Jewish. I was president of the club, but in 1933, before traveling to America, I resigned as president. This I did as a precaution, but the club members would not accept my resignation. So we agreed to postpone any decision until after my return. Conditions had so deteriorated by the time I came back that the administrators were thankful not to have to initiate a request for my resignation. Shortly after this, the club itself also vanished.

The municipality of Speyer had the questionable honor of being one of the first cities in Germany to forbid Jewish people from using the swimming facilities on the Rhine.

Mocking Caricatures and "Racial Disgrace"

Other cities followed suit at once. Many simple pleasures were forbidden.

"JEWS NOT WANTED!"

The disastrous events of recent years have brought a sudden upheaval with regard to the sense of worth and standing of the German Jews as citizens of the country. A world full of hope and resolve for the future has been shaken. Circumstances at present demonstrate with an elemental force the ongoing fate of the Jewish people. Again and again their hopes and aspirations have expanded in the course of time only to be followed by a sudden decline when circumstances left our people feeling rejected, pushed into a corner of life, into a world of resignation.

It was common to see signs on restaurants: "Jews not wanted." Jewish firms were identified through signs on store windows: "Jewish business," or files might have been kept on customers entering a firm by photographing these people as they entered. Such requirements, which became everyday fare in most villages, brought about the decline and eventual ruin of businesses operated by Jews and drove many to despair of making a living.

Two entrepreneurs whose business had been ruined, Paul and Käthe Moritz, from Speyer, traveled to Stuttgart to secure travel documents from the American consulate. The transaction proceeded in good order and the couple returned home to prepare for their trip. However a few days later, two officials from the state police showed up and demanded their passports be returned, stating the couple was to be subject to an investigation regarding a displacement of their property. All attempts to recover the passports failed. Eventually the couple returned to Stuttgart in hope of securing help through the consulate there but to no avail.

In the end they made their way to the lake, Wildparksee, outside the city. There, securing themselves to one another with strong ropes, they thrust themselves into the deep water. Shortly thereafter, a forest worker discovered the two and hauled their dead bodies onto the shore. There on the shore of the lake lay the man's hat as well as four letters addressed to relatives in which they expressed the despair that had driven them to their death. Just then, some Nazis came walking along and the forest worker exclaimed brashly:

"Look here! You're to be blamed for this!"

CHAPTER SEVEN

Driven from Home

Now it only remains for me to give an account of my last days and weeks in Germany. The reader will recall that the same day our "Beloved Child of the Pfalz" burned to the ground, all Jewish men of Speyer, age sixteen to seventy, were ripped away to Dachau. I was seventy-one and was not arrested.

Yet at five that evening an official of the Gestapo stomped into my home, demanding I leave the city and the Saarpfalz region by nightfall! My housekeeper, Fraülein Susanna Katten, who had served me for nineteen years, was also ordered to leave.

We had about one hour to pack the most necessary things: clothes, linens, and a few valuables. It was very hard for me to part from my home.

I had lived there for forty-seven years and had partaken in joys and sorrows with my family there. The unexpected nature of the move made it all the harder.

My flight was a sudden, distraught departure from the beloved town and home I would never see again.

Memories tugged at my heartstrings as I made abrupt preparations to part from home forever. Our home had been the envy of our neighbors on Landauerstrasse because of its location. Any time we needed a little diversion we could see everything that was going on through the front window. My sons particularly liked to keep an eye out for the high school professor Kessler, when he left his home in the mornings. From the quickness of his steps and the look on his face, they would get an idea of his mood and report on this that morning to the boys at school. Or they would enjoy estimating how large a coffee party Mrs. Meyer was having that day by the size of her cheesecake and the number of tarts she was carrying from the bakery. But those days were long past.

NAZI FRIENDS AND NEIGHBORS

Now we were forced to cope with only turmoil and distress. Yet two Nazi families living on the upper floor of my house brought some comfort by giving a helping hand to me and my housekeeper. I had gotten along well with these people for years. I knew both families were Nazis in name only. Each of them had aligned themselves with the NSDAP (National Socialist German Workers Party) to keep their jobs.

It was not easy to know where to go. One of my tenants urgently warned me not to flee to Mannheim, insisting it would be like fleeing out of the frying pan into the fire. Yet he failed to explain why he was so concerned, and that was where we, nonetheless, ended up going.

I called my friend from that city, Hch.[9] Freiberg, to ask him if we could spend the night with him. His daughter, Frau Jos. Rosenberger, answered the phone. She seemed surprised that I should have any hesitation about coming:

---

9. Hch. is an abbreviation for Haerel Check Haver, a title of honor in the Jewish community, meaning "the righteous one."

"Of course you're welcome! Our door is always open to you!" I heard her say.

But the next moment a stranger's voice addressed me from her end of the line:

"Mr. Waldbott, it will be all right. You can come here. I'll pick you up at the train station."

"But I won't be coming by train. I'll come by car."

"In that case be very careful! Don't stop anywhere in the city. Come directly to this house. I will meet you downstairs."

Who was this stranger? I felt uneasy about being met by an unknown party as well as his concern about my coming by car. Yet I wasn't ready to change my mind about traveling to Mannheim by taxi.

By this time all taxi-owners had been ordered not to transport Jews, but I still went ahead and called one. The driver was friendly and agreed to drive us to Mannheim:

"I will be at your home in a few minutes."

Fraülein Katten and I took our suitcases to the front door and waited. The others who helped us waited, too. But the taxi failed to come. After our boarders waited with us for at least half an hour, they bade us farewell and went back to their quarters.

The car still didn't arrive. I finally phoned to find out what had happened but no one at the taxi center could be of any help. Their driver had left the taxi base right after my call.

A full hour passed until the car finally appeared. Beside the driver of the cab sat an official from the Gestapo.

"I apologize, sir, for the delay. I had to first go to the appropriate office for a permit to drive you," the driver explained.

The police official then proceeded to question us:

"Where are you headed, Mr. Waldbott? ...What are you carrying in your suitcases? ...Let me see your documents!"

We answered his questions, one by one. He then looked through our papers thoroughly and, to our relief, added his stamp of approval. We drove the official back to the police station, he wished us a safe journey, and we were on our way!

THOUSANDS TO DACHAU

Our road led through Ludwigshafen and Mannheim, which are situated on the Rhine, with the river flowing through the towns. In both cities we drove past thousands and thousands of Jewish people lined up outside the railroad stations – people who had been arrested and brought by train to these points. From all over the Pfalz they were herded together to be packed into cattle cars and "crated" to the concentration camp of Dachau. People we knew who had recently traveled to Dachau and returned had reported that new barracks had been erected to receive huge numbers of Jewish prisoners. Their prison clothes would all bear the Jewish insignia, the Magen David.

No words can describe the pain we felt as we drove past these columns of our captured people, knowing a cruel destiny awaited these poor souls. Yet there was nothing we could do.

THE STRANGER

Mr. Freiberg, a charming and gracious retired businessman of seventy-five, was not there to receive us. When we arrived at his home, the stranger with whom I had talked and Mr. Freiberg's daughter, Frau Jos. Rosenberger, met us at the door. To my horror, the stranger who had invited us to come

Driven from Home

and spend the night wore a brown Nazi uniform. Another man in the house was dressed similarly in brown. Yet astonishingly neither of these two men showed hostility.

For whatever reason, these two Nazis had singled us out for an act of kindness at great personal risk. They were surely acting against the wishes of their superiors.

This is as much as I know: At eight A.M. two men in Nazi uniforms appeared at Mr. Freiberg's door. They created an impression of wanting to conduct a search of the apartment, but it was soon clear they were not bent on the sort of destruction taking place at that moment in many Jewish homes. Their intent was to protect the whole household and the property from attacks from without. They would stay until after midnight and would return repeatedly during the next few days and weeks to check up on our welfare.

When we finally began grasping what these two Nazis intended, we were comforted, but there were other concerns that first evening. When I asked why Mr. Freiberg wasn't at home, Frau Rosenberger replied:

"Papa was arrested earlier today. I don't know where they've taken him!"

The next few hours would be very trying for the young Frau Rosenberger as she anxiously awaited word of her father. We would later learn that Mr. Freiberg was being interrogated at that time along with three other men of his age in the town of Karlsruhe. It wasn't until far into the night that the Gestapo finally released their four hostages. My dear friend Mr. Freiberg did not arrive at the door of his home until three A.M., emotionally drained and physically exhausted.

His son-in-law, Mr. Henrik Rosenberger, had been the man the police were actually targeting. Propitiously for Mr. Rosenberger, this younger man had left on a trip early the same morning. The "enforcers of the law" had, nonetheless, felt obliged to arrest someone from the household and had taken Mr. Rosenberger's elderly father-in-law. Since the whole major action against the Jews of Mannheim was terminated about six o'clock on the evening of November 10, Mr. Rosenberger was fortunate enough to avoid being arrested.

Mr. Henrik Rosenberger's brother also lived in Mannheim, but he was less fortunate. This young man was secreted away to Dachau that same day and died there a few weeks later. It was said he died of a heart attack during a roll call in the prison. When his wife was informed of his death she traveled to Munich for the funeral. The bodies of an additional ten fellow sufferers were also buried simultaneously.

In spite of his good fortune on November 10, sadly Mr. Henrik Rosenberger met with death very early, succumbing suddenly to a kidney infection only a few months later. The worries of the time were largely responsible for the premature death of this young man.

JEWISH COMMUNITY STRIPPED

There in Mannheim we were informed about what had happened that day. The Nazis had been sent out to all parts of the city according to a well-organized plan. Two by two they apprehended the designated families, damaging all furniture, glass, porcelain, pictures, and whatever else they found. They threw everything through the windows, onto the streets, and set fire to the heaps of broken treasures. And the fire department, in full view of the flames and billowing smoke, did nothing.

Money and valuable documents were confiscated. It was said that these had not been included among the items

Driven from Home

ordered demolished and those responsible for destroying actual cash and original documents were later punished.

The huge Jewish community was stripped of every form of cultural activity. Every Jewish business in town was vandalized and reduced to rubble. A Jewish restaurant as well as the clubhouse of the Jewish Cultural Association, with its theater and auditorium, were destroyed, and the best-known German theaters, the National Theater, famous from classical times, and the Neue Rosengarten Theater, were all declared off-limits to Jews. Only two synagogue buildings were not set aflame, as they stood adjacent to a row of private homes that might also have caught fire. Everything movable in the synagogues, including chests with the Torah scrolls, was carried into the street and ignited. The beautiful hall at the cemetery was blown up by dynamite.

The entire populace had followed all this destruction and frequently one heard horrified exclamations over the (so-called) "heroic deeds" such as, "We are ashamed to be Germans!"

"JEWS WILL NOT BE SERVED"

A few days after the devastation in Mannheim, all grocery stores began to display signs with the words "Jews will not be served." Many of the store owners, nonetheless, delivered groceries to Jewish homes. Clearly, it was not the common people but higher authorities who bore the responsibility for these unthinkable deeds. After a few days the signs disappeared again from the windows and the doors of businesses. Storekeepers were simply refusing to display them.

During my stay in Mannheim I had an excellent opportunity to talk with fellow sufferers from other towns in southern Germany. Our conversations centered on the events of

CRYSTAL FRAGMENTS

November 10. From every direction we heard reports of the destruction of synagogues. In some places the order had gone out the previous summer, and these houses of God had already been destroyed.

Across from the main synagogue in Munich stood the House of the Artists, a home and a clubhouse for artists and art connoisseurs. The building had been renovated the previous summer and several high-class restaurants erected.

Hitler had been present at the dedication of the newly furnished art center. I was told by a reliable friend that he took one look at the synagogue across the street and exclaimed, "This blemish has to disappear at once!"

A few days later, workers arrived and began destroying the magnificent structure. Only administration buildings and the living quarters of the teachers and cantors were left standing. And these, too, were burned down on November 10.

TORAH SCROLLS BURNED

The synagogue in Nürnberg and the beautifully constructed synagogue of Kaiserslautern, built in 1886, were also destroyed in the summer of 1938. In the town of Dettelbach, near Würzburg, there was a large Jewish congregation. On the infamous date of November 10, 1938, the mayor of the city called on the caretaker, demanding the key to the synagogue and asking the caretaker to come with him. This man then awakened a teacher living nearby and asked him to come along. Once all three were inside the synagogue, the mayor walked directly to the holy chest and began burning the curtains.

"What are you doing?!" asked the caretaker, dismayed.

The mayor replied in a pathetic voice:

Driven from Home

"At this hour all synagogues of the Reich are being burned down."

I have recently learned about an experience of a Jewish schoolboy in Stuttgart at that time. This boy was Otto Hess, and he was the only Jewish student at the high school. The morning after the unthinkable destruction, he overheard a conversation among his school friends. One was blaming the Jews for the fury that had broken out among the population that night. Then another boy, the son of the fire chief, defiantly rose to the occasion:

> "No! I know more about this than any of you! My father was ordered to come to Ludwigsburg with the fire engine at two A.M. When they arrived there wasn't any fire. Then the building was set alight."

Similar stories were told to me from other towns.

ARYAN SUPERIORITY

I can report on another incident from the school days of this same Otto Hess. When he was in the fifth grade, Hess was tall, blond, and good-looking. One of his school subjects was Aryan Superiority. When this course was being taught, the principal gave permission to any Jewish pupil to be excused from the classroom. Professor Dr. Fischer, who taught the subject, told Hess he could leave the room, but the boy chose to stay and listen to the lesson. This is what he heard:

"Jews are small in size and fat. They have crooked noses, black eyes, and black hair."

At this some of the pupils called out:

"Professor, that's not true! Look at Hess!"

Another time Professor Fischer expressed himself this way: "Hess, there is something wrong in your family. Either your mother or your father are of Aryan origin."

One heard such statements daily.

How different from this man's approach was the attitude of a young colleague in Speyer who taught his pupils the same subject. He introduced the matter with these words: "Children, I am required to tell you something about the Jews. I want you to know in advance that this is not my own viewpoint. I have gotten to know Jewish people in an entirely different way. Yet I am required to tell it this way."

During my stay in Mannheim, a friend who now lives in Detroit told me about his relative Adolf Baer, an eighty-four-year-old Jewish man from Wimpfen on the Neckar River. He was a highly honored person who had been president of the local military club for forty years and who, on his eightieth birthday, had been showered with gifts from the "Christian" population of the city. The Duke of Hessen had even sent him congratulations. A few days after November 10, this man was arrested and sent to Dachau. Three weeks later the family received the ashes of their deceased father.

"THEY THREW ME OUT"

I stayed with my friends in Mannheim for five weeks until all my preparations had been made for my trip. My housekeeper was unable to travel with me due to her high registry number – the number that Jewish persons received on their applications to leave the country, indicating the order in which they could depart.

She remained behind for three months and was then able to travel to London. In May 1939 the remaining members of the Rosenberger-Freiberg family were able to travel to England, and shortly thereafter they, too, immigrated to America.

A few days after my arrival in Mannheim I asked for permission to return to Speyer to attend to my affairs with the local finance office and the state police. I needed a document granting me permission to emigrate to the United States, and it would be necessary to go to many different offices to obtain this certification of my clear record with all the authorities. At the finance office I was informed I was to be charged the tax on Jews to the amount of RM 5,400, twenty percent of the hypothetical value of my home. Since I didn't have the cash, I was told to go to an assessor and apply for a mortgage to be made out in favor of the finance office.

EMPTY POCKETS AND EMPTY HANDS

At the government finance office I gave notice that I would be leaving on December 16 and moving to the United States. The next day I received a letter from the German government informing me that to emigrate I would need the necessary permit from the government. At first they threw me out, but I persisted and returned. This time I was told to file a request for the appropriate permit.

A few days later I received the good news from the Bavarian Finance Office informing me that the permit would be granted. At the same time I was also told that the government of the Pfalz had been requested to send my pension every month to a special account in a foreign exchange bank. This plan was adhered to but only for the first six months of 1939. About this time, the finance office levied a tax on my pension as well as on the rental income from my house. From

CRYSTAL FRAGMENTS

July 1, 1939, my tenant informed me that my pension never came to me any more at all.[10]

As regards my actual departure for America, the tax on Jews had been raised by that time to RM 1,350. After paying this sum, the money remaining in my account was just enough to cover the cost of my trip. Thus, like my fellow sufferers, I had to leave the beloved homeland stripped of all I possessed.

Two days before I left, I traveled to the American consulate in Stuttgart, where my permit to immigrate to the United States would be issued. I spent the night at Hotel Reichsbahn, the only hotel accommodating Jews. When I entered the hotel I had an unpleasant surprise. A letter informed me:

> "Non-Aryans are asked to take their breakfast and other meals in their rooms."

I had intended to visit the Restaurant Bloch, the only Jewish restaurant in Stuttgart, but I was told the building had been completely destroyed on November 10. The owner would have to rebuild the building and his entire business with his own money.

At the consulate my papers were found in order and I received my visa quickly. The next day I departed from Mannheim and traveled to Bremen to begin my fifteenth crossing of the Atlantic Ocean, probably the last one of my life, with empty pockets and empty hands.

---

10. The check was still being sent to that address.

CHAPTER EIGHT

Boarding a Friendly Ship

Ultimately
I boarded
a friendly ship
for a land across the sea,
penniless but peaceably,
after a narrow brush
with treachery.
Yet some brown-shirts
protected me.

– Betsy Ramsay, 2006

In the end I was successful in boarding a German passenger liner. This ship represented part of the fleet of the North German Lloyd Company and was bound for New York City. There the fabled Statue of Liberty would be standing at the gateway with a torch in her hand as an emblem of freedom.

The trip was as pleasant as it was restful – a world apart from the trauma and agonies so many of our people were suffering. Nothing smacked of anti-Jewish sentiment.

On board ship I asked the chief steward, "How can this be possible on a German ship?"

His answer: "Aboard ship we know no differences. We only know passengers."

Clearly the winds had shifted, and we who were Jewish stood together on deck inhaling a fresh breeze of fair treatment.

With every ripple of the sea thoughts of the suffering of our people seemed further away. Yet they stubbornly remained on the horizon, and I had ample time to soberly consider the ongoing, step-by-step erosion of our rights as German citizens.

The matter of depriving Jews from holding state public office was one such step. During the early years of the Nazi regime many rules and regulations were directed at keeping Jews out of administrative positions and all public office. In practice, only members of the NSDAP were allowed to hold office in the service of the state. Other officials were permitted only to retain positions they already held.

Jews who had formerly held public office for the state were now permanently unemployed. The state was seeking to make a total separation between the races. It became necessary to prove one's Aryan origin in order to obtain any position in public office. The same applied to active military duty, work in public schools, work in blue collar jobs, or even in order to operate a farm. Thus, *fear of the authorities* thrust huge numbers into a position of dependency on those in power.

Through laws that had begun to be enacted in 1933, the German population was to "be forged into a single racial entity." In all matters of culture, the press, the arts, the sciences, the theater, the film industry, and the school system, Jews were not considered fit to participate and were excluded. German radio stations no longer presented compositions by

Boarding a Friendly Ship

Mendelsohn or Offenbach. One of the most popular poems by Heinrich Heine, "the Lorelei," still appeared in school books but with the attribution "author unknown."

The Nürnberg Laws went into effect from September 1935 and essentially deprived Jews of all rights and powers of citizenship. Jews became dependents of the state, and Jewish children were excluded from the public schools. Beginning in 1936 Jewish schools began to be formed, especially in the larger cities. These were also attended by children from mixed marriages. Conditions for starting such a school demanded a minimum of twenty pupils, however it was not always possible to gather this many Jewish children, even by combining pupils from several communities. Consequently, some Jewish children were not able to attend school at all.

Wherever Jews were concerned, the press operated under the dictated "guidance" of the Gestapo. The law for "protection of German blood and German honor" also came into effect in 1935, forbidding marriages between Jews and Aryans. Sexual intimacy between Jews and Aryans became punishable by death. Therefore, couples who had lived together in a mixed marriage for decades began to go separate ways. The Aryan husband and children of such a marriage experienced so many difficulties that the wife, out of love and concern, would often pressure her husband for a divorce.

From January 1, 1936, Germans or racially equivalent female citizens under the age of forty-five were no longer permitted to work in a Jewish household, and Jews were forbidden to fly the nation's flag.[11]

---

11. This law was passed due to the risk of a young German woman either becoming pregnant or developing a relationship with a Jewish man

The boycott against Jewish businessmen started at once in the beginning of the Nazi reign. It was hard to enforce this measure in the beginning since the people were not used to having their freedoms curtailed. However this goal was attained after five or six years as constant pressure was exerted against consumers. Little by little, Jewish businesses disappeared. Most entrepreneurs became impoverished if they didn't understand at the right moment that it was time to pull up stakes and leave the country.

The government of the Third Reich knew well how to take over the wealth of the Jews. They were not included in any tax breaks, and special high taxes were created, for example, the 20 percent tax on Jews intended as a punishment for the murder of a German legislator in Paris. Later an additional 5 percent was added to this tax.

During the early years, a certain portion of Jewish assets could be transferred to a foreign country, but the charges for these transfers in the form of an "escape-from-the-nation" tax were very high. In time this option, too, disappeared. Currently all immigrants come to the land of their refuge without money, and nearly every one of them must go on welfare.

Apart from the painful memories of all we had experienced during this step-by-step erosion of our rights as citizens, the trip passed peacefully. It was a welcome change to feel the salty spray blowing in my hair and not having to worry each moment about some new, disturbing event.

Within little more than a week we reached the American shore and my family was there waiting. Upon disembarking from the ship I also departed from German territory. I understood this meant I was parting from Germany, doubtless, for the rest of my life.

SOME STOOD UP FOR OUR PEOPLE

Now I have come to the end of my report, and I will close by only briefly reviewing what I have wanted to demonstrate. We should remember that in the time of the German monarchy and in the days of the Republic, after World War I, the Jews of Germany could feel like free men and citizens of a constitutional state. From the days after the Franco-Prussian War (1870–71), when the Jews enjoyed their rights and performed their duties as citizens, all restrictions on the rights of citizens because of religious differences were removed.

As long as a person lived his life within the framework of the laws of the land, freedom of thought and belief, as well as the right to choose one's own field of employment, were guaranteed. Every citizen, Jews included, had the self-evident right to enjoy the benefits of the state to the fullest and to be an asset to the state according to his ability. Private property was an unassailable asset.

Medieval despotic practices had disappeared whereby an individual could be condemned to the loss of his rights, often because of religious convictions. One could rightfully speak of the new time of enlightenment, which became a blessing not only to the Jews but to the people as a whole.

Hundreds of years earlier, during the time of the Crusaders in Germany, with their perverted persecutions of Jewish people, there were outstanding men who stood up for us. Bishop Rüdinger was such a man. A document concerning this bishop kept in the archives of the Pfalz in Speyer and dated September 13, 1084, is reminiscent of a situation similar to ours today. In comparing that period with our own, the horror-ridden phenomenon of the Hitler regime must never be considered representative of Germany in its basic character. I'm sure today there would be prominent voices raised in support of the Jews too, if the consequences were not as dire.

In more recent times, when brutal hostility was practiced against the Jews about the turn of the last century, there were, nonetheless, those who stood up on behalf of our people. Jews and their writings were being viciously attacked through the age-old practices: by gatherings of the populace throughout the nation, from the pulpit and the academic world, by fliers and brochures and in the daily papers. Not only those being attacked but also a number of Christian men took a stand against the ugly insinuations. The Emperor Friedrich III called anti-Semitism "the shame of the century." This is his proclamation of March 12, 1888, which breathed a spirit of tolerance:

> "Just as religious tolerance has been a basic principle in my house for hundreds of years, I want to grant protection to all of my subjects regardless of their religious views. Every one of them is equally close to my heart, as every one has equally given of himself in times of danger."

In the year 1891, five hundred of the most prominent men of science, administration, politics, industry, and trade signed a call to form a union against anti-Semitism. I will quote a few sentences from this document, because it places the Hitler period in its proper light:

> "A vicious fight continues to be waged against our fellow Jewish citizens. These actions are against the nature of our nation and its historic development as well as its position among all civilized nations.... The Jews, who are entitled to full and equal rights

as all other citizens, are subjected to the most ignominious insults in the newspapers and through mass distributions of fliers. Just because they are Jews they are persecuted and designated as outsiders and a threat to the moral foundations of the state and society. The goal of the anti-Semitic agitation is the abolition of the equal rights granted by the state. To participate in this or to watch this happen without taking any action would be a tragic oversight. German nobility and statesmen have condemned the disastrous and un-Christian actions of anti-Semitism. For the German people and particularly for Christians, it is a matter of honor above all else to bring this to an end as soon as possible."

Numerous highly esteemed Christian men became part of this united effort. Many clergy and writers whose writings were regularly distributed participated. Powerful speakers put down many public gatherings which attacked the Jews, working effectively to stem the tide of burgeoning anti-Semitic currents. The Jews themselves drew closer at this time in order to preserve their position as citizens and their social rights. Yet all these efforts were dealt their death blow with a single stroke on January 30, 1933, when the fate of the Fatherland fell into the hands of the Hitler regime.

THE WORDS OF A WISE MAN

Here in Detroit, my place of refuge, news from Germany is sparse. Friends back in Germany would never be allowed to bring me up-to-date on matters of interest to me personally.

However, six months ago, sadly, I received a letter from one of my friends in Speyer, who wrote:

CRYSTAL FRAGMENTS

> "The one enjoyment left to me, my daily walks through the cathedral grounds approaching the Rhine, have now been removed by municipal decree."

It's now more than a year since I began living in this large automobile city that has become a place of refuge for me and many others. Among them are many of my old acquaintances and friends as well as a large number of my former students. On certain days of the year I can meet with them in my house. As a matter of course we reminisce over events and experiences of bygone days. During such times I feel transported back into the past, sitting in front of my classroom again. The pupils listen attentively to my words:

> "We want to try and forget all the sad events of the last few years. We need to forget the heavy pressures we were subjected to and how we lost our rights.
>
> With a clean conscience we can say it was not our fault. It came about through the hatred that rose up and blamed us for being born to a Jewish mother. Let us so much more remember the old days, the years of our youth, when we could feel we were free citizens of a blessed state. In those days we could be active in all areas of society.
>
> Such a backward look can guide and fortify us with hope for a joyful future in a free land – a land that welcomed us when we were destitute. With thankful hearts we all intend to serve this country with respect for the law with all our physical and intellectual powers. Through all of this we need to remember an admonishment given us thousands

of years ago by a wise man. He was speaking to his people of that day who had been forced to leave their homes and live in a foreign land:

> 'Build ye houses and dwell in them; and plant gardens and eat the fruit of them… and seek the peace of the city whither I have caused you to be carried away captive…for in the peace thereof shall ye have peace' (Jeremiah 29:5–8)."

APPENDIX I

Cornerstone-Laying Ceremony

SEPTEMBER 29, 1912

(additional details)

The cornerstone-laying ceremony was attended by an impressive number of dignitaries, and other important persons sent their acknowledgments. Festivities began with a choral piece by the 18th Infantry Regiment band. Next, Mayor Wand of Neustadt enthusiastically welcomed this first step toward construction of the home calling it, "an honorable memorial for the entire citizenry."

Following the ceremony, a reception was held in the great hall of the "Saalbau". Three hundred and eighty people participated – a larger group than any such gathering previously reported in the history of the City of Neustadt.

The Chairman of the committee for the home, Dr. Reis of Speyer, initiated a series of speeches. He offered a toast to the Prince Regent, Luitpold of Bavaria, who always showed that all his subjects were equally dear to him when visiting the Pfalz. A telegram was also sent to the Regent that was graciously acknowledged.

Next, Dr. Dryfuss of Kaiserlauten gave a lengthy speech in which he thanked the City of Neustadt for the gift of the property and for this proof of their courtesy and willingness to cooperate at any time. Dr. Dryfuss was given the appointment of regional and district court physician only a few days earlier.

After a short intermission during which the military band contributed an artful presentation directed by Mr. Lill Eric Hafgren, head of the Conservatory of Music, the Mayor delivered the next speech. Speaking for the second time that day, again he heartily welcomed the plans to build the home. During the dinner that followed, many telegrams arrived bringing well wishes from, among others, the government counsellor, Mr. Buhl, and the representative of the Legislature in Munich, Dr. Hammerschmidt.

APPENDIX II

The Dedication Ceremony

MAY 10, 1914

(additional details)

The weeks following the memorable occasion of dedicating the foundation stone were filled with endless tasks for all involved. During numerous council meetings and inspection tours, the foremost goal was to always consider the most reasonable offers by capable companies and, wherever possible, to give preference to local entrepreneurs.

With the understanding, prudent and tireless leadership of the supervisor and head nurse, Carola Adler, the home was opened on April 1, 1914. A richness of activity began to take place in and around the home, as preparations progressed for the long-awaited day of the May 10 dedication ceremony. This day crowned six years of work by the Jewish people of the Pfalz in an enterprise in which all had participated.

Mayor Wand and district council member, Junker, were among the 530 guests at the dedication dinner in the festively decorated "Saalbau" hall. First the mayor addressed the assembled gathering. He began by thanking the administration of the city for their invitation to attend the celebration and then welcomed the hundreds of people present – many more than had attended the first celebration in September, 1912.

He extended special greetings to the honored president of the committee, Mr. Sigmund Herz, and to Dr. Reis, as well as to the entire leadership group and to all present. He referred, in his welcome speech, to those who would live in the home, emphasizing that they were every bit as important as other citizens. (Lively applause!) He then indicated that if anything more were said on this festive occasion, it would be superfluous – as he put it, "simply adding water to wine!"

He expressed what was in everybody's heart – Jews and Christians alike. This magnificent building, he continued, is a memorial to tolerance and neighborly love; that the people of Neustadt have cause to express thanks to the leadership group, in particular, for accepting the offer to put this marvelous building here. Most of all he thanked the president of the Hebrew congregation in Neustadt, Mr. Emil Behr, for his outstanding efforts in connection with the erection of the building and for showing concern both for the interests of the association and for those of the city and its workers.

The Dedication Ceremony

Top row: George and Edith Waldbott (left) and George's brother, Emil Waldbott (right); Bottom row: Leo Waldbott flanked by his two grandsons, Lee (left) and Richard (right), both sons of Emil

George and Edith Waldbott on their fiftieth wedding anniversary

Leo Waldbott (first to left in front row) with teacher colleagues at annual reunion

The Jewish home for the elderly on no.119 Karolinenstrasse, as seen from the street

The Dedication Ceremony

The dining room of the original home

The home as seen from the back

CRYSTAL FRAGMENTS

The home after it was burned down

The new home for the Jewish elderly, rebuilt after the war

ABOUT THE AUTHOR

Betsy Ramsay began freelancing as a journalist in the 1970s, and numerous English and Swedish publications have carried her articles. In 1976 she helped establish a news service in Stockholm, Sweden, which she headed for three years. Later she became managing editor for a small Swedish magazine, *Riksdagsbulletinen* (The Parliamentary Bulletin) from 1979 to 1986.

While in Sweden, Ramsay also taught English, German, and French as a substitute in public schools. In addition, she taught beginning Swedish to immigrants and wrote and produced short plays for children in Swedish within the framework of a children's drama club.

After moving to Israel in the fall of 1987, she continued to freelance as a journalist as well as tutor students privately in English language. She also taught English to weak students in the public schools.

Ms. Ramsay has previously published three children's books: *Footsteps* (Minerva Press, London, England, 1995), which appeared simultaneously in Swedish (Dagenförlaget, 1995), *The Burning Light* (Pitspopany Press, New York, 2002), and *Cecil Centipede's Career* (Author House Publishers, 2006).

She has also published three books of original poetry: *The Armor of Light* (Arthur H. Stockwell Ltd., Devon, England, 1974), *Handfuls of Grain* (Master Productions, San Diego, 1983), and *Honung Och Vete* (Honey and Wheat, Quality Office, Sweden, 2001). Her poems have appeared in a number of anthologies: *Voices From Israel* (Belle Terre Press, Jefferson, NY, 1998), *Voices Israel* 2000, 2003, 2004 (an annual publication of the Voices Group of Poets in Israel), and during her college years in *America Sings* (1952) and *Poetry* (Wellesley, Massachusetts, 1953).